# The Baseball
## TALMUD

# *The* *Baseball*

# TALMUD

## THE DEFINITIVE POSITION-BY-POSITION
## RANKING OF BASEBALL'S CHOSEN PLAYERS

*Howard Megdal*

**HARPER**

*An Imprint of HarperCollinsPublishers*
www.harpercollins.com

HarperCollins books may be purchased for educational, business, or sales promotional use. For information, please write: Special Markets Department, HarperCollins Publishers, 10 East 53rd Street, New York, NY 10022.

*Designed by Renato Stanisic*

All photographs by George Brace except for p. 154, Shawn Green, by Pete Borriello.

Library of Congress Cataloging-in-Publication Data

Megdal, Howard.
    The baseball Talmud : The definitive position-by-position ranking of baseball's chosen players / Howard Megdal with illustrations by George Brace. — 1st ed.
        p. cm.
    ISBN-13: 978-0-06-155843-6
    1. Jewish baseball players—United States—Biography. 2. Jewish baseball players—United States—History. 3. Baseball—United States—Statistics. 4. Baseball—Records—United States. I. Title.
    GV865.A1M44   2009
    796.357092'2—dc22
    [B]                                                                   2008040534

    10 11 12 13   OV/RRD   10 9 8 7 6 5 4

*For Rachel: More than anything,*
*more today than yesterday,*
*more in paperback than in hardcover.*

# CONTENTS

# INTRODUCTION

If there's one thing Jews like to do, it's argue. Many of you reading this book are nodding sagely in agreement. Some of you, however, rose to your feet indignantly to dispute my blatant generalization. Either way, my point is proven.

Our passions are often brought to bear on the great issues of the day facing our people. What will be done to bring about peace for Israel? How do we resolve the fundamental questions of what Judaism will be in the 21st century? Is intermarriage something to embrace, or will it tear our community apart forever?

But our ardor is not limited. I first conceived the idea for this book during a trip to the batting cages with members of my college intramural softball team. A good friend of mine who is sabermetrically inclined (and a Member of the Tribe) had recently concluded that the most valuable Jewish player in major league history was Hank Greenberg, not Sandy Koufax.

Our center fielder, a Jewish sociology professor, reacted as if my friend had defended supermarket challah. The normally mild-mannered line-drive hitter left decorum behind to shout about Koufax's dominance and left the car in utter disbelief, cursing under his breath.

I realized that I could never hope to solve the vital questions that will challenge Jewish scholars for generations to come. But I thought it was imperative to get a sense of our place in baseball history. There is far more to Jewish baseball players than simply Greenberg's slugging and Koufax's (eventually) masterful control. The story also includes the Yiddish Curver and the Rabbi of Swat. It touches on historical figures like John McGraw and Franklin Delano Roosevelt. It is the story of the Miracle Mets of 1969 and the earliest professional baseball played.

Modern advances in both research and the sabermetric movement allow me to create a more definitive ranking of Jewish baseball players than ever before. A search for how contemporaries viewed even the oldest players is now available with a few mouse clicks. And both major and minor league stats are readily available and can be contextualized for both era and park. This is a golden age for baseball research.

Following my overall top 10, I have ranked every Jewish player known at the time of publication by position. This provides a more complete context of each player's value, beyond merely offensive statistics, to the relative, and previously undefined, values within that player's position. While it is often difficult to compare the apples of catchers to the oranges of relief pitchers, pitting players against their own position provides, I believe, a clarity to each player's value.

I elected for as expansive a definition of Jewish as possible—any player who self-identified as Jewish qualified. David Newhan, for instance, is a Messianic Jew—that is, to many, a Jew for Jesus. He said he found Jesus during his performance and injury struggles in 2002–2003, and mentioned his time at Pepperdine University, a Jesuit school, as a leading force in his conversion. However, Newhan still celebrates Passover and Hanukkah, and considers himself Jewish.

Ultimately, that is good enough for me, as is a player whose father is Jewish, or one who converted. I am a baseball expert, not a Judaism expert. Many will not consider Newhan Jewish because he accepted Jesus Christ as his personal lord and savior. Others will not consider me Jewish because I am an infrequent participant in synagogue services. Still others will consider my wife an apostate because of her persistent refusal to eat corned beef or pastrami when we visit Katz's Delicatessen. I will leave it to the religious scholars to debate Newhan's Judaism.

Overall, as of July 25, 2008, there had been 16,696 players, and fewer than 160 of them were Jewish. For a country that is approximately 3 percent Jewish, this is low—less than 1 percent of all major leaguers.

Therefore, I am sure of one thing: we as the Jewish people cannot afford to cast aside middle infielders. Were Newhan a relief pitcher, perhaps it would be different. But at second base, we need all the Chosen People we can get.

I expect that in the tradition of my ancestors, there will be virulent responses to my rankings, and counterarguments to them, until this becomes a diamond-inspired Talmud for our national pastime.

There will come a time when a young Jewish player, fresh off his first major league game, will be interviewed and say, "I'm hoping to be Al Rosen good—but I'll settle for being Goody Rosen good."

And thanks to this book, we'll all know exactly what he means.

# 1

## The Greatest Jewish Baseball Player

### 1. Hank Greenberg

There is broad consensus on who the two best Jewish players in major league history are—Hank Greenberg and Sandy Koufax. But the confusion over which player is the best is perfectly understandable—the two performances are very close, and while the players played two very different positions, their careers mirror each other.

Greenberg was a power-hitting first baseman in the best offensive era in baseball history, the 1930s. Koufax was a power pitcher in the best pitching era in baseball history, the 1960s. Greenberg's career numbers were limited by World War II. Koufax's career numbers were limited by injury that caused his retirement at age 30.

So how do we go about determining which elite player

is better? Baseball Prospectus's WARP3, which determines season value in terms of wins over a replacement-level player, adjusted for park and era, is an important tool. Through this metric, we see that Koufax put up a career total of 68.3 wins over replacement player in 12 seasons, with his first 6 seasons totaling 13.9 wins, and his final 6 seasons totaling 54.4 wins.

Greenberg, meanwhile was at 77.0 wins in his career over 12 seasons (plus one at bat in 1930). Greenberg was a valuable player from the start and posted a season of eight wins in 1934, his second full year, at age 23. So for a greater portion of his career, Greenberg was an elite player.

But the question becomes, was Koufax better in his prime to balance things out? The answer is: not really. Match up their best seasons, and you get the following:
Koufax: 11.9, 10.6, 10.3, 8.2, 7.7, 5.7, 3.7, 3.5
Greenberg: 10.5, 9.8, 9.7, 9.6, 9.2, 8.0, 6.6, 5.5

While Koufax's 1966 stands a bit above anything Greenberg did, the next few best seasons are pretty indistinguishable—and Greenberg simply had more of them.

## 2. Sandy Koufax

There is, amazingly enough, a statistical argument to be made for Lou Boudreau over Sandy Koufax. But there are a couple of factors that make me discount the edge Boudreau would have.

Boudreau's WARP3 values are astounding—he had a 15.7 WARP3 in 1948, his signature season. And this was not as flukish as you'd expect—he also posted seasons at

12.1, 12.0, 12.0, and 11.8. His career total of 110.1 dwarfs Koufax's 68.3.

But this total is built on a pair of adjustments I simply can't buy. One is giving Boudreau enormous credit for playing in Cleveland Stadium. Baseball Prospectus takes his career line of .295/.380/.415 (batting average/on-base percentage/slugging percentage) and inflates it to .301/.376/.479. The power numbers, in particular, look suspect to me—Cleveland Stadium was a pitcher's park, but not to that extreme. Baseball-Reference.com neutralizes Boudreau's line to an improved .299/.385/.420—better, but not ludicrously so.

His WARP3 is also inflated by tremendous fielding stats—Baseball Prospectus has him saving 161 runs over replacement in his career. Now, fielding stats are still improving in legitimacy for current players, where we have real-time play-by-play to evaluate each player by computerized zones. Still, there are holes in the data. The '40s defensive stats? Not even close. So I'm supposed to buy into Boudreau saving nearly 100 more runs in his career than Omar Vizquel, who is at 69? I just can't credit him with all of that.

Put him in a more appropriate context, and Boudreau is still a Hall of Famer, a very valuable player. But he pales in comparison to Koufax, whose dominance is unquestioned and whose strikeouts are completely verifiable.

### 3. Lou Boudreau

Now Boudreau, according to Baseball Prospectus, put up an EQA (offensive production expressed as an average) of

.290. That ties him with Shawn Green, who also posted an EQA of .290. Green also did so in a career approximately 14 percent longer—7,082 at bats for Green to 6,029 at bats for Boudreau.

But Boudreau holds the edge for several reasons. For one thing, Boudreau was an elite player for a larger portion of his career. Green's best seasons all came between the ages of 26 and 30; Boudreau had Hall of Fame seasons between the ages of 22 and 30.

Another edge is positional. Green was, for much of his career, a good outfielder. But that value simply pales in comparison to the value of a good shortstop. While it is reasonable to speculate about the true level of Boudreau's defensive contributions, no one has suggested that he wasn't an elite defensive shortstop. When the two players are similar offensively—Boudreau and Green also had identical career OPS+ marks (on-base percentage plus slugging percentage adjusted for era and park, and expressed relative to average) of 120—the tie has to go to the shortstop.

## 4. Shawn Green

I am tempted to say Green holds the advantage over Buddy Myer simply because he reads Eastern philosophy—indeed, my conversation with Green about the philosophical treatise *Siddartha* in 2007 was my only time discussing the book in a major league clubhouse, though in fairness to other players, I rarely bring it up.

But Green in fact holds an edge for his contributions on the field: his .290 EQA and 120 OPS+ are considerably ahead of Buddy Myer's .273 and 108, respectively.

Injuries really kept Green from the upper-tier discussion—in his three best seasons, he posted WARP3 marks of 11.8, 11.3, and 9.8, with plus defensive marks in all three seasons.

## 5. Buddy Myer

For Myer, a combination of consistency and longevity places him in the top five, even though Al Rosen is better known. Such is the case when in the shadow of home run hitters.

There is little question that, at his best, Rosen was a better player than Myer—OPS+ edge of 137 to 108, EQA of .302 to .273. But Rosen, limited by back problems, had just 3,725 career at bats, while Myer was at 7,038.

To rank Rosen above Myer, it would be necessary to come to the conclusion that Rosen was *twice* the player Myer was. And there's just not evidence enough to support that.

Myer was underrated in his own time for two reasons: one, he did not hit home runs, and two, there wasn't the understanding of the importance of on-base percentage. Take Myer's age-30 season of 1934. His .305 average did not rank in the top 10, but his .419 on-base percentage was sixth in the American League, thanks to 102 walks. For a hitter that presented virtually no power threat (he hit 38 career home runs, and just 3 in 1934), that total is astounding.

## 6. Al Rosen

Al Rosen's career is astounding as well—despite logging just seven full seasons, and five healthy ones, he isn't far from Hall of Fame consideration.

Consider that Rosen's career OPS+ of 137 is not far off of Mike Schmidt's 147 or Eddie Mathews's 143—both considered the best to ever play third base. Rosen's decline phase is included in his total, of course, and isn't averaged out by a longer peak due to his back injuries.

His is a similar story to that of Ralph Kiner, who played just 10 seasons but made the Hall of Fame with his 369 home runs. But Kiner was an outfielder—Rosen played an above-average third base. Add positional adjustment, and Rosen likely makes the Hall with just another two or three healthy seasons. The number of players who can punch a ticket to Cooperstown with such a short career are very few—and that, more than anything else, speaks to Rosen's dominance.

It also places him above Sid Gordon, a very good player, but one whose offense falls a bit short of Rosen's, and who certainly did not provide a glove equal to Rosen's at third base.

## 7. Sid Gordon

Gordon's offensive contributions were quite impressive, even underrated at the time, because, much like Myer, a large portion of his value was tied up in his ability to draw a walk. (This is a recurring theme for so many Jewish players—unlike Eliot Spitzer, they grasped the value of not paying for something they could get for free.)

Gordon's career OPS+ was 129, and his EQA was .301—a tribute to his career. But worth noting also is that his OPS+ was 107 or higher for nine straight seasons after he returned from serving in World War II—indeed, it was 121 or higher for seven seasons from 1948 to 1955. That sustained excellence places him above Ken Holtzman, a talented pitcher, but one who simply didn't perform at that high level. Holtzman had just two WARP3 seasons above 5.5; from 1948 to 1953, Gordon never dropped below 6.3.

### 8. Ken Holtzman

Holtzman did, however, provide a ton of seasons with good value in his 15 major league years. His WARP3 career total of 51.6 ranks him ahead of both Harry Danning and Mike Lieberthal.

While Holtzman was not an elite player for most of his career, he was a valuable member of a starting rotation far more often than not. In seven seasons, his WARP3 was 4.4 or higher; in six seasons, his ERA+ was better than the league average. (The ERA+ stat adjusts a raw ERA for park and era, relative to the league average—100 being average—so a score of 105 would be expressed ERA+5, meaning 5 percent better than league average.)

### 9. Harry Danning

Danning and Lieberthal had nearly identical careers—in essence, Danning gets the tiebreaker because he fought the Nazis. Indeed, Lieberthal had 4,218 at bats, Danning just

2,971, or nearly 30 percent fewer at bats. Yet in WARP3, Danning had a career total of 39.9, while Lieberthal was at 46.5—a difference of just over 14 percent. When both were healthy, Danning was simply the better player—and by enough of a margin to overcome Lieberthal's longevity edge.

## 10. Mike Lieberthal

Lieberthal's edge over some of the top young Jewish players in the game may be fleeting. His career EQA is .266 (entering 2009, Ryan Braun's is .311, Ian Kinsler's is .297, and Kevin Youkilis's is .297), enough to overtake any positional advantage Lieberthal enjoys as a catcher, particularly in light of the terrific defense Youkilis plays at first base.

Still, none of them are close to Lieberthal's career WARP3 of 46.5; Youkilis is closest, at 27.1. Each player will need to perform at his current level for another three to five seasons to approach Lieberthal on the list.

| NAME | GAMES | AT BATS/INNINGS | OPS+/ERA+ | WARP3 |
|---|---|---|---|---|
| 1. Hank Greenberg | 1394 | 5193 | 158 | 77.0 |
| 2. Sandy Koufax | 397 | 2324.3 | 131 | 68.3 |
| 3. Lou Boudreau | 1646 | 6029 | 120 | 110.1 |
| 4. Shawn Green | 1951 | 7082 | 120 | 82.9 |
| 5. Buddy Myer | 1923 | 7038 | 108 | 75.8 |
| 6. Al Rosen | 1044 | 3725 | 137 | 53.1 |
| 7. Sid Gordon | 1475 | 4992 | 129 | 63.6 |
| 8. Ken Holtzman | 451 | 2867.3 | 105 | 51.6 |
| 9. Harry Danning | 890 | 2971 | 104 | 39.9 |
| 10. Mike Lieberthal | 1212 | 4218 | 101 | 46.5 |

## FEARLESS PREDICTION: OVERALL, 2019

1. Hank Greenberg
2. Sandy Koufax
3. Ryan Braun
4. Lou Boudreau
5. Shawn Green
6. Kevin Youkilis
7. Ian Kinsler
8. Buddy Myer
9. Al Rosen
10. Sid Gordon

# 2

## *Catcher*

For a people who pride themselves on intelligence and education, donning the so-called Tools of Ignorance would seem to be a fool's errand. Indeed, I was forbidden to play catcher in Little League by my mother, and it is hard to imagine a Jewish matriarch willingly agreeing to let her precious Morris or Sol repeatedly sit in front of blazing fastballs, sly, deceitful curveballs, or even deceptively dangerous knuckleballs. (One can imagine a Jewish mother's response to Bob Uecker's advice for catching a knuckleball: "What if it starts moving again? Let someone else pick it up!")

Nevertheless, the position has provided the Jews with some of our greatest players. While other positions are littered with obscurity, many of our catchers have been both productive and well known.

The best at this position is essentially a toss-up between

*Harry Danning*

Harry Danning and Mike Lieberthal, two gifted offensive players at a position where hitting is at a premium. Defensive stalwarts like Steve Yeager, Brad Ausmus, Jeff Newman, and Joe Ginsberg also provided their teams with quality service behind the plate. Moe Berg, linguist and spy, is in a class all his own.

### 1. Harry Danning
*Bats Right, Throws Right*
*New York Giants, 1933–1942*

Danning gets the nod despite very similar production to Mike Lieberthal. They were also both California products, though Lieberthal grew up in upscale Glendale, Danning in a working-class Mexican-American Los Angeles neighborhood. His first team was a semipro outfit, sponsored by a Mexican grocery, and 95 percent of his teammates reportedly spoke little to no English.

He debuted in 1933 for a New York Giants team that was desperate for a Jewish star and box office attraction. Both he and fellow Semite Phil Weintraub were spare parts for the pennant-winning Giants, who were managed by first-year skipper Bill Terry (who had taken over after John McGraw's 30-year run).

Danning had the misfortune of being stuck behind All-Star Gus Mancuso until 1937, playing sporadically on Giants teams that won two pennants and at least 90 games each year. Danning finally broke through on the 1937 Giants team that lost to the Yankees in the World Series, hitting

.288 with a .438 slugging percentage in 292 at bats. That performance was enough to earn him a 14th-place finish in MVP voting and Gus a permanent seat on the bench (he was traded after the 1938 season).

Though the Giants slipped to third in 1938, Danning improved his batting average to .306 while slugging an identical .438, placing 16th in MVP voting despite the Giants' finish.

Danning got better and better, though his teammates, best among them an aging Carl Hubbell and unprotected Mel Ott, did not provide enough support to keep the Giants from sliding to fourth and then sixth place in 1939–1940. Despite the poor team records, Danning finished in the top 10 of National League MVP voting both years, a clear indicator that his outstanding play was not lost on observers.

While Danning did not hit a ton of home runs (only 29 over the two years), his offensive contribution was significant. Not only did he hit over .300, get on base roughly 35 percent of the time, and slug higher than .450 both years, but he did so in over 500 at bats each year. No other catcher, not even Hall of Famer Ernie Lombardi, slugged as high as .400 in as many as 400 at bats each season. Danning's combination of durability and success made him the preeminent catcher in these two years.

Like many players, his career was cut short by serving in World War II, though arguably the amount of games caught had taken its toll by the time he enlisted after the 1942 season; both his '41 and '42 efforts were not nearly as good as 1939–1940. But as often happens in All-Star selections, his star power was enough to get him on the team in 1941, his fourth and last selection. He did not play after the war and retired to Valparaiso, Indiana.

By all accounts, Danning had a terrific sense of humor. A story about him: after Ted Williams won the 1941 All-Star Game with a long home run, Danning (who was catching) was asked by losing pitcher Claude Passeau where the pitch had been.

"I can't tell you where it was," Danning said. "But I can tell you where it is."

Danning might have added to his career numbers had Hitler not intervened—he certainly would have done so had Gus Mancuso not intervened. Despite both, he is our finest catcher, the man we as a people will rely on in the eventual cosmic baseball tournament between religions.

### 2. Mike Liberthal

*Bats Right, Throws Right*
*Philadelphia Phillies, 1994–2006*
*Los Angeles Dodgers, 2007*

After spending a first-round draft pick on Mike Liberthal, the Phillies had reason to believe they were watching the development of a star when in his first full season, he hit 20 home runs at age 25. However, like many of his teammates on that 1997 Phillies team, along with the fortunes of the team itself, stardom, and October success, ultimately remained elusive.

Lieberthal followed with an injury-plagued 1998, but in 1999 he had easily the greatest season of any Jewish catcher, and one of the finest campaigns by any catcher, even *goyim*. He hit .300, with an on-base percentage of .363 and a slugging percentage of .551 on the strength of 31 home runs and 33 doubles. He also was awarded a Gold Glove for his defensive efforts, which included a 100-game errorless streak. At age 27, it seemed as if he was set to battle Mike Piazza for National League All-Star slots well into the 21st century.

Unfortunately, his body betrayed him. He appeared in 131 or fewer games (out of a possible 162) in each season through 2006. He signed on with the Dodgers for 2007, but backing up the young, sturdy Russell Martin is no way to top that number, and he finished his career with just 77 at bats and a lone RBI.

After calling it quits in June 2008, Lieberthal would seem to have a good case for GJB (Greatest Jewish Backstop): most home runs (150), highest RBI (610), and a career slugging percentage of .446. Danning's numbers are 57, 397, and .415. Lieberthal also had about 1,000 more at bats. However, it is hard to hold this against Danning. For one thing, any chance he had of playing after 1942 was eliminated by World War II. While in the service, he was told by an army doctor that his knee was "shot."

By means of comparison, Mike Lieberthal was carried off the field May 12, 2001, with a torn anterior cruciate ligament. His ACL was replaced by a graft taken from a cadaver. A continuous passive motion machine hooked up to his bed allowed him to rehabilitate as he slept. His daily isometrics (modern strength training) and comprehensive physical therapy also helped him to return in time for the start of the 2002 season.

"Cadavers, screws, an hour-and-a-half surgery," Lieberthal told *USA Today* in 2001. "Now it seems like players come back from anything."

Danning's injury was not so severe that he couldn't serve in the armed forces. His examination consisted of an army doctor using a slang term. Lieberthal, meanwhile, recovered in months from an injury he couldn't even stand on.

My point? How do you penalize a guy for being too busy fighting World War II to play baseball and for being born too soon to enjoy modern medical miracles?

Lieberthal also played in a far richer offensive era, when extra-base hits were as plentiful as the corned beef at the Second Avenue Deli. By contrast, home runs for a prewar catcher were as sparse as the number of times my mother has thrown caution to the wind. Baseball Prospectus's Equivalent Average, which expresses total offensive production as a batting average, has Danning with a career mark of .270, narrowly edging Lieberthal's .269. Add to that Danning's standing in the MVP vote of his time and service in World War II (arguably, had Danning and the Allies not prevailed, Lieberthal would never have gotten the chance to play), and Harry the Horse gets the edge.

### 3. Brad Ausmus

*Bats Right, Throws Right*
*San Diego Padres, 1993–1996*
*Detroit Tigers, 1996*
*Houston Astros, 1997–1998*
*Detroit Tigers, 1999–2000*
*Houston Astros, 2001–*

But for expansion, Dartmouth-educated Brad Ausmus could have been the great Jewish frontline player New York has craved since John McGraw signed Mose Solomon to be the "Rabbi of Swat" in 1923. A 48th-round pick of the Yankees in 1987, Ausmus was selected instead in the expansion draft to stock the Colorado Rockies for the 1993 season.

Ausmus never played for the Rockies either, getting dealt to the Padres. It was a feeling he would need to get used to— he was traded by the Padres, and by the Astros, along with getting dealt twice by the Tigers (although, unlike fellow catcher Harry Chiti, he was never exchanged for himself).

Despite an undistinguished offensive career, Ausmus has made a living with his defense and durability. Through the 2008 season, he caught 474 of 1,337 would-be base stealers, a success rate of over 35 percent, while playing in at least 125 games every year from 1996 to 2006, including 150 for the 2000 Tigers.

Another refreshing thing about Ausmus is that no one has ever accused him of taking steroids. His career-high home runs (9) is for the 1999 Tigers. The power spike, combined with his defensive excellence, earned him a spot on the All-Star team that year.

Respect has come slowly to Ausmus, who, despite his excellent work behind the plate, did not win his first Gold Glove until age 32 with the Astros in 2001. As often happens with Gold Glove groupthink, he then quickly nabbed his second in 2002, and another in 2006. Like Steve Yeager, Ausmus saw much action in October, playing the role of starting catcher for five postseason Astros teams, and making his World Series debut in 2005. His career postseason line of .245/.304/.377 isn't far from his overall career numbers of .255/.328/.353.

In a different era, Ausmus might have been considered one of the greats. But with base stealing deemphasized and power considered the key, a catcher who prevents thefts and provides little pop is less valuable than ever. The trade by the Yankees robbed Ausmus of his chance to shine before millions of his own religion, and Lieberthal's gaudy offensive numbers overshadowed him even among his own faith and position. Perhaps in this day and age, good defensive catchers are meant to be seen and not heard.

Ausmus gets the nod over Steve Yeager, though like the top two guys, Ausmus and Yeager are very close. Ultimately, they were very much the same player, with Yeager's .244 career EQA edging Ausmus's .240, but Ausmus's durability far outpacing Yeager's (only two years with more than 117 games, and only five seasons topping 100).

Ausmus also gets extra credit: his maternal grandfather was a rabbi.

## 4. Steve Yeager
*Bats Right, Throws Right*
*Los Angeles Dodgers, 1972–1985*
*Seattle Mariners, 1986*

Steve Yeager is a favorite of mine. He was one of the few Members of the Tribe to receive Hall of Fame votes (2 in 1992). He was the cousin of an astronaut (Chuck Yeager), an area where, like the national pastime, Jews do not have the presence we have in, say, the legal profession. And he was a terrific defender, catching 365 of 960 would-be base stealers (38 percent). His offensive totals are also undervalued by virtue of playing in a poor offensive era and one of the best pitcher's parks (Dodger Stadium) in baseball history.

Yeager was drafted by the Dodgers in the fourth round of the 1967 draft and debuted in 1972. After a strong 94-game stint in 1974 (.266 with 12 homers in 316 at bats and solid defense), he took over full-time from Joe Ferguson in 1975. He went on to hit double figures in home runs six times in his career, though batting average became his offensive Achilles' heel (he hit over .228 just once in his last six seasons).

Managers Walter Alston and Tommy Lasorda considered Yeager's offense a bonus; however, they were thrilled with his defensive prowess. It is hard to argue with the results: in his 15 seasons, Yeager's teams captured six division championships, four pennants, and a World Series title in 1981.

A closer look at the stats would indicate that Yeager was more than incidental to his teams' successes. His batting, on-base, and slugging percentages were .228, .298, and .355

in the regular season; he raised those to .252, .317, and .449 in the postseason (remember, in October players face better pitching, making that jump even more impressive).

He became particularly prodigious on baseball's biggest stage: in 58 World Series at bats, he hit .298, with a slugging percentage of .579. His 1981 October Classic performance earned him a share of the World Series Most Valuable Player award. Not bad for a defense-first catcher.

The argument for Yeager as GJB is closer than it would appear—basically, if you value defensive catchers and World Series MVPs very, very highly, he is your man. However, with both Danning and Lieberthal excelling defensively for at least part of their careers, the overall edge at the plate (for point of reference, Yeager's career EQA is just .244) is too great.

However, Yeager continues to hold two records: most career home runs by any Jewish catcher or player who posed for *Playgirl* (102) and most consecutive *Major League* films acted in by a former World Series MVP (3, if *Major League III: Back to the Minors* starring Scott Bakula can be considered a film. Why they found it necessary to bring back Yeager, but not, say, Charlie Sheen or Rene Russo is beyond me. At least the "Hats for Bats" guy is around for the third one.)

Yeager was also an innovator in the area of safety, inventing the catcher's neck protector, unsurprising, since any Jewish person knows the importance of being safe and protecting one's voice.

## 5. Jeff Newman

*Bats Right, Throws Right*
*Oakland Athletics, 1976–1982*
*Boston Red Sox, 1983–1984*

No one will ever confuse Jeff Newman with the predecessors on this list. The top two played at a star level; the next two were good enough to start for championship teams. But Jeff Newman had two very marketable skills that kept him in the big leagues for nine years.

The flashier skill was hitting home runs. Newman hit 9 of them in 268 at bats in 1978, then socked 22 in 1979, and followed that with another 15 in 1980. Unfortunately, he had no other corresponding offensive skills, with an inability to take a walk (just 70 over those three years and 1,222 at bats) combining most unfortunately with batting averages of .239, 231, and .233. As a result, 1980 was his last as a regular.

He did stick around for another few years, largely on the strength of his glove. Newman threw out 160 of 406 attempted base stealers, a career percentage of nearly 40 percent, and in his first two big league seasons stealing on Newman was a worse-than-even proposition.

In this time of praise for on-base percentage, many would view Jeff Newman and his career .264 mark (to go along with an equally ugly .224 batting average) as a scourge upon their team, a kind of Jewish Miguel Olivo. But at a position where any offensive value at all is about as rare as anywhere on the diamond, Newman was, well, better than Joe Ginsberg.

### 6. Joe Ginsberg

*Bats Left, Throws Right*
*Detroit Tigers, 1948–1953*
*Cleveland Indians, 1953–1954*
*Kansas City Athletics, 1956*
*Baltimore Orioles, 1956–1960*
*Chicago White Sox, 1960–1961*
*Boston Red Sox, 1961*
*New York Mets, 1962*

Without stolen base/caught stealing numbers from Ginsberg's time, it is hard to evaluate him defensively. He had a good reputation, certainly, and sticking around for 14 years is to his defensive credit, since he wasn't in the big leagues for his potent bat (career .241/.332/.320). But there seems to be some rule where catchers who can't hit are universally assumed to be great defensive players and given a free pass into the backup catcher club.

For instance, Ginsberg's most comparable player, according to the Web site Baseball-Reference.com, is Jorge Fabregas. Now, when I went to Shea Stadium for the first time late in the 1998 season, I was excited to see Mike Piazza, whom the Mets had acquired earlier in the year. But it was a day game after a night game, so I didn't. I saw Jorge Fabregas.

So maybe I'm biased. But Fabregas, who couldn't hit a lick, was also a terrible fielder. I'm assuming he bounced from team to team that saw him not hit and made the same faulty assumption: "This guy must be one hell of a fielder."

Now, I'm not saying Ginsberg wasn't really a fantastic fielder. He might have been: that was his reputation. But we know how good Jeff Newman was at throwing out runners—with Ginsberg, we can only speculate.

Ginsberg, unlike Ausmus and Yeager, also does not get extra credit for playing for championship teams. He played for losing teams throughout his career, in 10 of 14 seasons, and in three of the four years he didn't, he played a grand total of 49 games. He was traded from one losing team to another, except in 1954, when he belonged to the Cleveland Indians, who won 111 games. The Tribe, perhaps fearing he'd become disoriented at the top of the standings, gave him just two at bats, then quickly shipped him to the Pacific Coast League.

Ginsberg was able to shine there for the Seattle Rainiers in 1955, hitting .290 as their starting catcher and leading them to the PCL title. However, his success bred a return to major league also-random, when he was purchased by MLB's closest proximity to a farm team, the Kansas City Athletics. His career continued in that vein, finishing with 5 at bats for the 1962 Mets, the losingest team of them all.

### 7. Moe Berg
*Bats Right, Throws Right*
*Brooklyn Dodgers, 1923*
*Chicago White Sox, 1926–1930*
*Cleveland Indians, 1931*

*Washington Senators, 1932–1934*
*Cleveland Indians, 1934*
*Boston Red Sox, 1935–1939*

It's hard to add anything to the legend of Moe Berg, backup catcher, spy, and linguist, though certainly not in that order. I suspect that no one would have been more excited to use the Internet than Berg; the man collected so many newspapers that wherever he was living would have piles of them stacked high on his floor. He was an information junkie before the information age.

As a player, Berg was said to have originated the label "good-field, no-hit," and justifiably so. His career line of .243/.278/.299 was, amusingly enough, accumulated during an extreme hitters' era; his true offensive value was below that. Still, he was perceived as valuable enough to stick around for 16 seasons in professional baseball, though again, much of that allure was due to the belief that he could, and did, teach much to his teammates. His career high in at bats was 352, and he topped 200 at bats only one other time in 16 years.

But Berg was more than simply smart for a baseball player. In a sport where merely getting caught reading a book, regardless of its author, gets a player tagged with a virtual monocle, Berg put off returning to the Dodgers for spring training 1924 in order to complete his studies at the Sorbonne. He was added to the first major league baseball touring team in 1934 because he could speak Japanese like a native. He served as a panelist on the radio quiz show

*Information Please*, which served as a broadcast version of the Algonquin Round Table (with many crossover members) in the 1930s and '40s.

I think there's a case to be made that the things that kept him from a satisfying life probably held him back as a baseball player, too. He was easily bored, with his coaching work after retiring, even his spy work (he spent nearly two years with the Office of Strategic Services, a forerunner of today's CIA) and many of his other pursuits. (He got his law degree from Columbia University in 1925, but stopped practicing law after a single winter at it.)

Berg had excelled at Princeton University as a shortstop, and the Dodgers saw enough in him to give him regular time in 1923, when he was the youngest player in the majors, and asked him back in 1924. (That team, without him, went on to win 92 games, so it's not as if they were bereft of talent.)

One suspects that had Berg devoted more of himself to a single pursuit, the last 15 years of his life, in which he suffered from clinical depression, might have been happier. Had he focused on baseball, he also might have reflected on a far more successful baseball career. However, his failure to do so makes it hard to think of anyone, living or dead, who would be more interesting at a dinner party.

## 8. Norm Sherry

*Bats Right, Throws Right*
*Los Angeles Dodgers, 1959–1962*
*New York Mets, 1963*

Between his brother (Larry Sherry, the 1959 World Series MVP) and his protégé (Sandy Koufax, one of the great pitchers, kosher or *treif*), Norm Sherry had quite an impact on the world of baseball in general and Jewish baseball in particular during a short but sweet major league career.

Sherry, like Koufax a Brooklyn boy, signed with the Dodgers in 1950. However, he became a victim of a talented farm system organized by Branch Rickey and spent eight seasons in the minor leagues before getting to Los Angeles in 1959. Though he got into just two games, he was able to see his brother shut down the White Sox and help the Dodgers win their first post-betrayal-of-Brooklyn title.

While Sherry served as backup to the capable John Roseboro from 1960 to 1962 for the Dodgers, and managed a very impressive .283 average, .353 on-base percentage, and .503 slugging in 138 at bats in his first year (his subsequent production was not at this level), his largest contribution to the Dodgers, and indeed to baseball, was finally convincing a hard-throwing project named Sandy Koufax to take just a bit off his fastball in exchange for control during spring training in 1961. (Koufax, a bright man, had heard this many times before; it is quite possible the hitch Sherry corrected in Sandy's delivery also made a difference.) Koufax, who had considered quitting baseball after a lackluster 1960 season, set the single-season National League strikeout record for left-handers in 1961, a mark that stood until Koufax broke it again in 1963 and then a third time in 1965.

Sherry, meanwhile, did not find a similar path to stardom, hitting .256 and .182 behind the durable Roseboro, before he was sold to the New York Mets following the 1962 season.

Sherry played in a career-high 63 games for the 1963 Mets but batted just .136, thus ending his career. It also ended the automatic Jewish catcher's seat on the Mets bench he inherited from Joe Ginsberg when Sherry did not return in 1964 and Chris Cannizzaro failed to convert.

Sherry went on to manage for years in the Dodgers and Angels systems and briefly took the reins for the major league Halos in 1976–1977, where his success more closely mirrored his playing career than Koufax's. He went on to serve as pitching coach in Montreal, San Francisco, and elsewhere, with distinction, but like Orson Welles, he never reached the heights of his first masterpiece.

## 9. Jesse Levis

*Bats Left, Throws Right*
*Cleveland Indians, 1992–1995*
*Milwaukee Brewers, 1996–1998*
*Cleveland Indians, 1999*
*Milwaukee Brewers, 2001*

One thing our people have always been known for (sometimes with admiration, too often with negative overtones) has been the ability to know value. Why pay for something you can get for free?

Jesse Levis's career is a tribute to that principle, made most famous by my mother, who recently combined coupons, sales, and know-how to purchase a new pair of jeans from a prominent retailer for 44 cents. Levis, a batter without much power, still managed to find his way to first base quite a bit over the course of his career by taking walks, the buying wholesale of baseball hitting.

Levis, a Philadelphia product, was drafted by his hometown Phillies out of high school after earning all-county honors as a catcher his senior year (a lightly regarded Mike Piazza took the laurels at first base). He elected to attend the University of North Carolina rather than accept 36th-round money. The delay paid off, as he signed with Cleveland after the Indians made him a fourth-round pick three years later. (Piazza, meanwhile, played junior college ball and was a 62nd-round pick by the Dodgers—and only as a favor to his father, Vince, a friend of Tommy Lasorda's.)

Levis made his way up the organizational chain, posting relatively unremarkable stats along the way, with the exception of his ability to make contact and reach base for free. Each season until he reached the majors, Levis walked at least as often as he struck out, with his season high in strikeouts reaching a paltry 42. However, Cleveland's All-Star backstop, Sandy Alomar Jr., kept Levis from getting the opportunity to wow Cleveland's sizable Jewish population.

Finally, after a AAA season that could not be trivialized (.311 batting average, .411 on-base, and .454 slugging), Levis was shipped to the Milwaukee Brewers to serve as their catcher of the future. At age 27, it appeared Levis had finally arrived.

Unfortunately, although his on-base skills translated nicely, the rest of his game did not make the transition. His on-base percentages for the two seasons were a respectable .348 and .361, but his slugging numbers (.283 and .335) were far below par, and he threw out just 26 of 97 attempted base stealers (just under 27 percent).

Thus began a merry-go-round for Levis as an emergency backup catcher for hire, the guy who gets mentioned by announcers in the rare instance that both major league starter and backup fall victim to the injury bug. Levis garnered just 96 at bats in the big leagues over the final seven years of his career, while playing for the Devil Rays, Indians, Braves, Brewers, Reds, Phillies, and Mets organizations. He continued to judiciously weigh each errant pitch, finishing with a .380 career on-base percentage. Unfortunately, a foot injury befell him in a 2004 season that began with promise (he was hitting .370 at the time of the injury).

All in all, the man could judge pitches the way a Garment District tailor can judge good fabric. Unfortunately, he never could put together the whole suit.

## 10. Skip Jutze
*Bats Right, Throws Right*
*St. Louis Cardinals, 1972*
*Houston Astros, 1973–1976*
*Seattle Mariners, 1977*
Some people are born Jewish, and some people elect to become Jewish. It almost seems as if Skip Jutze, who was

born and raised as a *goy* despite the "Jew" syllable in his last name, had our faith thrust upon him. Growing up in Queens, peer pressure to don a yarmulke and consume gefilte fish must have been overwhelming, and Jutze eventually bowed to the inevitable and converted.

For reasons that are unclear, Jutze was drafted twice, in high rounds, before signing his third time around as a fourth-round pick of the St. Louis Cardinals. His .324 batting average and .455 slugging at AAA Tulsa earned him a cup of coffee in St. Louis in which he threw out 12 of 18 would-be base stealers. After the season, he was shipped to Houston in a four-player deal and received the bulk of the playing time for the 1973 Astros. He was a spectacular flop, however, batting .223 with no home runs. His defense was subpar as well—he nabbed just 20 of 61 potential thieves.

He seemed destined for a forgotten career with the Astros, accumulating 198 at bats over three seasons from 1974 to 1976, failing to hit very much, and allowing 48 of 65 base runners, an Enron-like environment for larceny. (See Fabregas, Jorge for more on why teams thought he was great defensively.) He had no home runs in his entire career through 1976.

Then the gods looked down upon Skip Jutze and cried out: Expansion! Jutze was traded to the newly created Seattle Mariners, who went ahead and started Skip on April 12, 1977. Unlike in his previous 547 major league at bats, Jutze finally got a pitch he could drive and produced the first home run in Seattle history. His place in the extensive Mariners' lore is secure, tucked neatly somewhere between Edgar Martinez's career, the 2001 campaign (regular season only), and that time George Costanza's father yelled about Jay Buhner.

Jutze rode his new power to the tune of three long balls in just 109 at bats. Then, knowing to quit while ahead, he retired after the Mariners released him in the spring of 1978.

However, like Joe Ginsberg's magical 1955 before him, Jutze proved that Seattle is a very hospitable place for Jewish catchers. One would hope that Mariners management will pick up on this trend—it is no accident the franchise has never even been to a World Series.

## 11. Eric Helfand
*Bats Left, Throws Right*
*Oakland Athletics, 1993–1995*
Drafted by the Oakland Athletics in the second round of the 1990 draft, he was supposed to be the next Gene Tenace. Needless to say, he wasn't.

Helfand didn't even hit much in the minors, save a breakout year at high-A Modesto (.289/.405/.470), but his defensive reputation and pedigree kept him moving up the chain. He finished with a career .171 batting average in the majors over 105 at bats, while hitting a respectable .250/.345/.390 in 1,353 minor league at bats.

Fortunately for the A's, they could afford a less-than-stellar second-round pick, because they had a can't-miss first-rounder that year: Todd Van Poppel (they left Chipper Jones for the Braves). It was a tough draft for the team with a history of drafting more Reggie Jacksons than Steve Chilcotts.

## 12. Ike Danning

*Bats Right, Throws Right*
*St. Louis Browns, 1928*

Ike Danning was the brother of Harry the Horse, and had anyone bothered, he could have been nicknamed "Ike the Ignored," though his 3-for-6 career gave him a batting average of .500, 133 points higher than the all-time career leader, Ty Cobb, though in 11,428 fewer at bats.

The Dannings were one of six sets of Jewish brothers to play in the major leagues. Ike was six years older, and overshadowed by his younger brother. Norm Sherry faced similar familial humiliation when Larry won the 1959 World Series MVP and, to add insult to injury, was his teammate at the time. (No telling if the Sherry parents would speak glowingly of Larry, then gesture in disgust to Norm and say, "And this one can't even hit a curveball.")

Danning had a stellar run in the minor leagues from 1926 to 1929, hitting between .285 and .330 each season, three of the four spent in the A-ball Eastern League. But Ike's six at bats of major league glory came with the 1928 St. Louis Browns, after being shipped with Mike Cvengros for Fred Fussell, who was nicknamed "Moonlight Ace." Apparently, everyone got a cool nickname but poor Ike. Moonlight Ace finished with a career ERA of 4.86 (being a Moonlight Ace isn't that helpful when the first major league night game takes place seven years after the end of your career). No word whether or not Moonlight Ace, like Buck O'Neil, eschewed bitterness and claimed he was "right on time."

## 13. Frank Charles
*Bats Right, Throws Right*
*Houston Astros, 2000*

Arguably the finest Jewish catcher in modern indy-league baseball, Frank Charles promised so much more when he was drafted in the 17th round out of Cal State Fullerton. Frank tore up the Northwest League, a low-A-level minor circuit, hitting .318/.377/.510 as a rookie. Though he was old for the league, it was an auspicious beginning.

The Giants handled him poorly, however, giving him just five A-ball at bats, then rushing him to high-A, where he struggled in San Jose, hitting .290, but with just a .322 on base and .353 slugging percentage. The Giants then quickly gave up on him, and he was signed by the St. Paul Saints, owned by Bill Veeck's son, Mike.

Frank did not excel particularly in the Northern League, but the Texas Rangers saw enough to sign him for the 1994 season. He reached AA, but Texas then promptly released him. The Giants gave him another try, but he got only 10 at bats at AAA Fresno, likely due to injury, and was released. His chances of reaching the big leagues were minuscule.

But after signing with Houston, and holding his own at AAA New Orleans in 2000, he made his way to the big club as a September call-up. On seemingly the only recent Houston team not to play meaningful September games (the 2000 edition finished 72–90), Charles managed three hits in seven at bats, good for an Ike Danning-esque .429 batting average.

He played several more seasons, even putting up a .300/.339/.495 line for the Northeast League's North Shore club, but he never made it back to the show. With catchers slow to develop, and the Giants quick to give up on him (not to mention their player development of the time was less than legendary), it is fair to wonder if Frank Charles might have had a better career in a different system.

### 14. Harry Chozen
*Bats Right, Throws Right*
*Cincinnati Reds, 1937*

Harry Chozen played 16 years in the minor leagues, and one solitary game in the big leagues, September 21, 1937, as one of the backup catchers to Ernie Lombardi, one of the few bright spots on an eighth-place team.

Chozen appears to be the leading argument for a Diaspora. Born to Ukrainian immigrants, he went on to a successful baseball career after a childhood in Winnebago, Minnesota, where reports incredibly claim his was the only Jewish family. San Antonio, Texas; Lake Charles, Louisiana; Albany, New York; Newport News, Virginia; Knoxville, Tennessee—these are just a sampling of the minimal-*matzoh* metropolises where Chozen thrived.

He retired to Lake Charles after his career was over, and the local college, McNeese State, named a baseball scholarship after he died. Hillel has no entry for McNeese State in its Jewish life on campus guide. Winnebago has apparently not changed, either: an Internet search for "Winnebago,

MN Jews" turned up nothing other than a JDate promise to "find Jewish singles in Winnebago, MN!" The search returned no results.

### 15. Bill Starr

*Bats Right, Throws Right*
*Washington Senators, 1935–1936*

Bill Starr made his name not as a player, but as a trailblazing executive. His playing career included 24 at bats with the 1935 Washington Senators, where he played alongside fellow Jew (and our all-time hits leader) Buddy Myer. Spurred by a clubhouse just eight short of a *minyan*, Myer hit a career-high .349 and finished fourth in the American League MVP voting despite playing for a sixth-place team. (Hank Greenberg won the award.) Starr hit .208, still good for second on the team among Jews.

He went on to play several more years in the Pacific Coast League (PCL), then both independent of major league baseball and considered the top minor league. In 1937, en route to hitting .219 for the then–minor league San Diego Padres, he pinch-hit for teammate Ted Williams (one can assume it is no coincidence that the manager's name has been forgotten by history). A broken leg ended his career at 28.

In 1944 he was part of a group that purchased the Padres, with Starr taking over day-to-day operations. He signed the league's first African-American ballplayer, John Ritchey. He then made a push to make the PCL a third major league, which seems far more ludicrous a proposition today than it did at the time. No baseball teams were west of St. Louis, and the level of baseball was not far off. (A similar 1961 effort, based on a league in New York, Denver, Minneapolis, Toronto, and Houston, called the Continental League, produced a deal with Major League Baseball to add the New York Mets and led to the naming of the Mets' stadium after the linchpin of the push, Bill Shea.) However, the PCL effort failed, and Starr sold his share in the Padres at a large profit in 1955.

Starr went on to become a successful real estate developer, and while no Moe Berg, Starr published a book contrasting modern baseball (it was published in 1989) with the baseball of his youth. As one would expect, he maintained that older players were more talented and were better at fundamentals and went on to criticize computer statistics, claiming they are no match for good, old-fashioned scouting. A sequel, in which he detailed walking uphill in the snow six miles to school each day, was never written; Mr. Starr passed away in 1991. Sadly, his book is out of print, and this successful baseball man is largely forgotten. Had his PCL gambit been successful, however, we might instead have loudly lamented the day Starr Stadium was renamed "Thompson's Water Seal Park."

### 16. Bob Berman

*Bats Right, Throws Right*
*Washington Senators, 1918*

While Bob Berman played just two games in June 1918

for the Washington Senators, his impact on the world was substantial, with the bloodiest months of World War I and an influenza outbreak that killed an estimated 25 million following his swings. One shudders to think what Berman would've wrought with three games.

| NAME | GAMES | AT BATS | OPS+ | WARP3 | Additional |
|---|---|---|---|---|---|
| 1. Harry Danning | 890 | 2971 | 104 | 39.9 | 4 All-Star |
| 2. Mike Lieberthal | 1210 | 4218 | 101 | 46.5 | 2 All-Star, 1 Gold Glove |
| 3. Brad Ausmus | 1914 | 6121 | 75 | 68.8 | 3 Gold Gloves |
| 4. Steve Yeager | 1269 | 3584 | 82 | 35.1 | 1981 WS MVP |
| 5. Jeff Newman | 735 | 2123 | 75 | 5.5 | 22 HR in 1979 |
| 6. Joe Ginsberg | 695 | 1716 | 79 | 6.7 | |
| 7. Moe Berg | 663 | 1813 | 49 | 4.0 | Spoke fluent Japanese |
| 8. Norm Sherry | 194 | 497 | 70 | 2.2 | Mentored Sandy Koufax |
| 9. Jesse Levis | 319 | 654 | 68 | 3.8 | |
| 10. Skip Jutze | 254 | 656 | 45 | –1.3 | |
| 11. Eric Helfand | 53 | 105 | 29 | 0.1 | Hit .315 in AAA, 1997 |
| 12. Ike Danning | 2 | 6 | 180 | 0.2 | .500 avg. in 6 at bats |
| 13. Frank Charles | 4 | 7 | 143 | 0.2 | |
| 14. Harry Chozen | 1 | 4 | 39 | — | |
| 15. Bill Starr | 13 | 24 | 9 | –0.1 | |
| 16. Bob Berman | 2 | 0 | — | — | |

# 3

## *First Base*

First base is a far thinner position for the Jewish people than catcher—just 10 Jews can be considered primarily first basemen, and one of them—Ron Blomberg—actually played more designated hitter than he did first base.

Frankly, however, with Hank Greenberg as the starter, not many backups are needed. Greenberg, a cultural icon, put up numbers that are historically great for any religion.

A distant second, but quite an accomplished player, was Mike Epstein. Current Red Sox first sacker Kevin Youkilis is threatening to take over Epstein's hold on runner-up. Blomberg not only played DH, he was the very first. Phil Weintraub had a solid career as well, while Lou Limmer found his greatest success in the minor leagues, and Greg Goossen found his in the movies.

*Hank Greenberg*

## 1. Hank Greenberg
*Bats Right, Throws Right*
*Detroit Tigers, 1930, 1933–1941, 1945–1946*
*Pittsburgh Pirates, 1947*

It's a well-known fact that the war cost Greenberg a large portion of his career. However, the wrist injury he suffered 12 games into the 1936 season, a recurrence of a malady from the 1935 World Series, cost him his age-25 season, right between hitting .328/.411/.628 at age 24 with 36 home runs and 170 RBI, and his age-26 campaign, when he hit .337/.436/.668 with 40 home runs and 183 RBI.

This was a serious hitter. His career slugging percentage ranks seventh all time, while his on-base plus slugging, or OPS, is eighth all time. Consider that his career is missing five peak years but contains all of his decline, and his rate stats are even more impressive. According to Baseball Prospectus's EQA, Greenberg was a .326 hitter. Albert Pujols, for instance, is at .334, Willie Mays is at .328, and Reggie Jackson comes in at .306.

Leaving aside his injury year of 1936, when he missed all but 12 games due to a broken wrist, and just providing Greenberg with credit for his four and a half years in World War II, he would have quickly climbed the ladder of the home run leaders. He hit 41 home runs in 1940, his last full season before the war. Assuming a downturn as he reached and passed 30—let's say an average of 35 home runs per season—he'd still have put up roughly another 160 to 170 home runs, which puts him right in the 490 to 500 career range. For comparison, Lou Gehrig hit 493 career home runs. Of course, Gehrig had 8,001 at bats, while Greenberg, even with those extra four-plus seasons, would have likely netted around 7,300. And remember, Gehrig retired as the second-best home run hitter of all time, trailing only Babe Ruth.

But measuring Greenberg has to move beyond simply baseball. For instance, through all of the Jackie Robinson festivities, a secondary point has frequently been made that, while the struggle to integrate baseball was unimaginably difficult, Brooklyn was the perfect place, politically and culturally, for such an endeavor to take place.

By contrast, the world, and in particular, the major league city that Hank Greenberg called home when he got to the big leagues, was arguably the toughest time and place a Jew could have gone to establish himself in the public eye. Greenberg got to Detroit to stay in 1933—the year Adolf Hitler took over in Germany. Detroit's most famous citizen, in fact the city's raison d'être, was Henry Ford. Ford published a newspaper that unceasingly railed against Jews, and a collection of the newspaper's columns was published in book form as *The International Jew—the World's Foremost Problem*. Reportedly, Hitler was one of his readers and admirers. Ford went on to blame "international Jewish bankers" for World War II after receiving the highest award a foreigner could receive from Hitler's government. (At least Ford was nice enough to suffer a heart attack when shown films of the Nazi concentration camps, according to a collaborator of his—I suppose it was the least he could do.)

Along with Ford's presence shadowing Greenberg's city was the leading voice of reactionary public Catholicism in the 1930s, the Reverend Charles Coughlin, whose weekly radio sermons were estimated to reach more than 40 million people at their peak. Coughlin pinned the Russian Revolution and the Great Depression on the Jewish people from his pulpit in Royal Oak, Michigan, just outside Detroit.

Into this situation, and a city ravaged by the Depression and looking for scapegoats, stepped Greenberg. One can only imagine the degree of difficulty. And even when he made good, there were not scores of Jews ready to join him—Robinson had a black teammate before the year was out, and African Americans were commonplace in baseball by the early '50s. Greenberg, for his career, was the symbol of the Jewish people and all that it entailed.

This is not to disparage what Jackie Robinson accomplished—of course, Robinson had a barrier of nearly 50 years to break, while other Jews had played in the major leagues around the time Greenberg came up. (John McGraw was desperate for a Jewish star, but Giants scouts had apparently dismissed the local boy Greenberg. Given their lack of success with the Jews they did sign, this is not surprising.) To attempt to quantify or compare what the two men did is impossible, and silly.

To Greenberg's credit, he often told his son that "he never knew what having it bad was until he saw how they treated Jackie Robinson," and Greenberg also was one of the first players to publicly offer encouragement to Jackie during Robinson's rookie year. The point is not to play the two men off each other; rather, the Robinson tale that is being told again and again is an incomplete one without the story of his immediate predecessor, Hank Greenberg.

## 2. Mike Epstein

*Bats Left, Throws Left*
*Baltimore Orioles, 1966–1967*
*Washington Senators, 1967–1971*
*Oakland Athletics, 1971–1972*
*Texas Rangers, 1973*
*California Angels, 1973–1974*

Typically, top prospects get overhyped. But in Mike Epstein's case, not only was his baseball prowess touted, his mental facility was the subject of press clippings. Even his physical resemblance to Mickey Mantle got him media attention.

Epstein, like Greenberg roughly 30 years before, was a Bronx product, though he played his high school ball across the country at Fairfax High School in Los Angeles. He was a multisport star, excelling in both baseball and football, though he gave up football to avoid injury. He became an All-American at Cal Berkeley, won a gold medal with the U.S. Olympic team in 1964, and was signed with a $20,000 bonus that same year by the Baltimore Orioles.

Even before his professional debut, Epstein was the subject of multiple items in *The Sporting News*. First, a young fan mistook him for Mickey Mantle in an airport and asked "Mr. Mantle" for his autograph.

"Obligingly, Epstein wrote, 'Mickey Mantle,'" *The Sporting News* reported in its March 20, 1965, issue. "'I didn't want to break the kid's heart,' he said."

Two weeks later, *The Sporting News* profiled "Egghead Epstein: The Slugging Scholar," as he prepared for his professional debut with Stockton of the California League.

"Writers need more than a pencil and paper when interviewing Epstein," Doug Brown wrote in the April 3, 1965, edition. "They need a reference library, as well, for they hear words like 'inculcate,' 'adversary,' 'self-image' and 'defeatist,' along with quotations from Emerson and Socrates." The story goes on to describe an Emerson quotation Epstein left for a friend who was considering giving up baseball.

Epstein quickly supplied professional results to go along with his intellectual and imitational skills. He hit 30 home runs to lead the California League in 1965, and his power led a rival manager to label him "Superjew," which has for some reason never been the name of a comic book.

His stock soared still higher after Epstein hit over .300 again in 1966, this time for AAA Rochester, with another 29 home runs.

"He reminds me of a giant bomb waiting to go off," Orioles farm director Harry Dalton said. "He's a kid who could hit 50 home runs."

But the Orioles soon sent that bomb down the Potomac, trading Epstein to Washington for pitcher Pete Reichert. Epstein now found himself in a cavernous ballpark in the heart of the biggest pitchers' era in baseball history.

His power numbers continued to impress, though the batting average did not stay above .300. Epstein hit 9, 13, 30, and 20 home runs from 1967 to 1970, though his batting averages were more pedestrian .229, .234, .278, and .256. But his secondary numbers were particularly impressive, as Epstein drew plenty of walks, leading to on-base percentages of .331, .338, .414, and .371.

Epstein's 1969 was particularly noteworthy—he finished 25th in the MVP voting for a team that finished in fourth place. He finished ninth in home runs, though in just 403 at bats (he was fourth in the league in home runs per at bat and fifth in OPS). His season EQA of .334 was identical to Henry Aaron's 1969 mark.

At age 28 in 1971, Epstein seemed poised to become a star. But as the Senators often did, they found it expedient to deal Epstein (and reliever Darold Knowles) to Oakland for Don Minchner, Paul Lindblad, Frank Fernandez, and Washington's favorite trading target, cash.

Epstein picked up right where he'd left off in Oakland, hitting for power and reaching base a ton, even though he'd been sent to an even bigger pitcher's park, the Oakland Coliseum. His .234/.368/.438 line with 18 home runs in 328 at bats was still good enough for third on the team in both long balls and slugging percentage. The A's were no slouch team, either, winning 101 games and the American League West.

He followed that performance with an even stronger 1972, posting a .270/.376/.490 line with 26 home runs in a career-high 455 at bats for the 1972 World Series champions.

He even hit .284 against left-handed pitching, a career-long bugaboo for Epstein, though his power (22 of 26 homers) came against right-handers.

But owner Charlie Finley of the A's was never one to stand pat, and he acquired a new catcher, Ray Fosse, who had yet to be pronounced "finished" by his collision with Pete Rose in the 1971 All-Star Game. That left the young Gene Tenace without a position. And Tenace was a low-average, high-walk, high-power hitter ready to play first base for less money—leaving Epstein without a position. He was dumped to the Texas Rangers, newly arrived from their former life as the Washington Senators, for reliever Horacio Piña.

Because life is never fair, Epstein found himself in another pitcher's park, Arlington Stadium. He was given just 85 at bats before being discarded again, this time to the California Angels. But his swing didn't return right away, and by May 4, 1974, he was released by the Angels.

A rendering of Epstein's career suggests that he was never fully appreciated in his time. If an Epstein were to find his way to the major leagues today, sabermetric disciples all over the country would be clamoring for him, given his secondary skills like drawing walks. And in a hitters' era, Epstein likely would have posted numbers too strong to ignore—let alone ones that allowed him to go from starting first baseman on a world champion to out of baseball in just 18 months.

Baseball-Reference.com has a "neutralize stats" button, which adjusts a hitter's or pitcher's stats to both a neutral era and a neutral park setting. Through this lens, Epstein's true value becomes much clearer. He finished his career with a .244 average, a .358 on-base percentage, and a .424 slugging percentage—good numbers, but nothing earth-shattering. Put him in a neutral setting, and the line rises to .267/.387/.466, or roughly speaking, Carlos Beltran's career line with more walks. (In Coors Field, he'd have hit 40 homers twice and posted a .318/.446/.553 career line—Larry Walker territory.) His career EQA of .294 ranks ahead of players like Dale Murphy, Tino Martinez, and Robin Ventura.

Epstein became a wandering coach, teaching hitting to minor leaguers in both the San Diego and Milwaukee systems, and currently runs a hitting school and stars in a DVD on the subject. Hopefully, at long last, those who purchase his product are able to look past his career batting average and see that the sum of his contributions as a hitter were quite good, if not super. But as Emerson wrote, "To be great is to be misunderstood."

### 3. Kevin Youkilis
*Bats Right, Throws Right*
*Boston Red Sox, 2004–*
The crown jewel of Boston general manager Theo Epstein's attempt to create a team of Jewish supermen (he maxed out at 4 in 2006, 1 short of the major league record, 6 short of a *minyan*, and 21 short of the Yeshiva varsity unit), Youkilis showed in 2007 and 2008 that his successful 2006 was no fluke and has established himself as a legitimate bat at first

base for a championship team. He cemented those gains, and added to them, as the starting first baseman for the 2008 American League All-Star team.

Born and raised in Cincinnati, Youkilis stayed home for college at the University of Cincinnati, where he set records for home runs, slugging percentage, walks, and on-base percentage.

He was picked up in the eighth round of the 2001 draft by the Red Sox and continued his walking ways. He tied a minor league record by reaching base safely in 71 straight games, and as he climbed the organizational ladder, Athletics general manager Billy Beane reportedly coveted him. A number of conversations from Michael Lewis's book on Beane, *Moneyball*, detail the extent of Beane's lust for a Youkilis trade.

However, the Red Sox held on to him, and are glad they did. While he didn't hit for much power in the minor leagues, he managed to add it to his game, separating him from the Dave Magadan comparisons that followed him for much of his career. Mags was a good major league player, but without any pop, he failed to stick at his two positions, first and third base, as a regular.

Not only can Youkilis also play second base and left field, he already slugged .429 in 2006, a mark 52 points higher than Magadan's career mark, and lifted that mark to .453 in 2007. He then batted .500 in the ALCS against Cleveland, leading the Red Sox back from a 3–1 deficit and into the World Series.

It is indeed early to be asking questions about Youkilis's Hall of Fame chances, but two factors should be considered moving forward. The first will be what Boston does with Youkilis. Should they return him to third base, and keep him there, his chances improve considerably, particularly since his defense is solid at the position. His offensive contributions there will stand out far more than they will at first. (Should they move him to second, he'd have an even better chance, but the Sox seem set up the middle for a while with Dustin Pedroia at second and Jed Lowrie at shortstop.) Of course, considering that he won the Gold Glove at first base, a long career filled with doubles and walks might be enough to get him in as well.

But the price Youkilis has paid for coming up onto a veteran, talented team like Boston is a late start to his career as a regular. His first full season, 2006, came at age 27, and his first superstar season at age 28. (By contrast, Jose Reyes won't turn 27 until June 2010—his eighth season in the big leagues.) A healthy career could allow him the 10 seasons of production he'd need to be in the discussion (getting him to, say, 2,200 to 2,300 hits by age 38), but that is asking a lot. More likely he has a peak roughly as long as top Jewish third baseman Al Rosen, who lost the front end of his career to World War II and the Indians' refusal to play him over Ken Keltner.

Of note for the hordes of Jewish mother/daughter combos swarming Fenway Park in the hope of snagging Youkilis— his nickname is promising, "the Jewish Greek God of

Walks." But daughters, beware: Red Sox manager Terry Francona told the *Boston Globe* in 2006, "I've seen Youkilis in the shower, and I wouldn't call him the Greek god of anything."

### 4. Ron Blomberg

*Bats Left, Throws Right*
*New York Yankees, 1969, 1971–1976*
*Chicago White Sox, 1978*

The ironic part of Ron Blomberg being primarily remembered for his role as baseball's first-ever designated hitter is that his athletic profile runs entirely counter to the general perception of the oafish, one-dimensional ballplayer we've come to associate with the position.

Blomberg was a multisport star at Druid Hills High School in Atlanta, earning *Parade* All-American honors in baseball, basketball, and football. He received 125 college basketball scholarship offers, even drawing a recruiting visit from UCLA's John Wooden. Football was no different—he got 100 gridiron scholarship offers as well.

His first mention in *The Sporting News* was May 20, 1967—for his running: "Another highly regarded prospect is Ron Blomberg, a right-handed throwing and left-handed hitting first baseman . . . whom most of the ivory hunters say can 'do it all.' Blomberg has been clocked in 3.8 seconds going from home plate to first base."

He was the top overall pick in the 1967 draft, going ahead of future big league standouts Jon Matlack, John Mayberry,

Ted Simmons, and Bobby Grich. Just over two years later, he made his way to New York for a brief call-up. Two years later, he was up to stay.

His minor league tenure was similar to his major league career—he hit very well when healthy, but injuries were a problem he never could conquer. His minor league slugging percentage was .461, with two seasons above .500, but his season-high in home runs was just 19, because his season-high at bats was a mere 384.

The 1971 Yankees were a team in transition. Blomberg easily supplanted Danny Cater at first base, while young stars like catcher Thurman Munson and center fielder Bobby Murcer (who hit .331 with 25 home runs, drawing comparisons to Mantle in the process) seemed to portend success just ahead.

But after Blomberg's rookie season, a spectacular debut by any measure (.322 average, 7 home runs in 199 at bats, good for a .477 slugging percentage), the Yanks went out and got 37-year-old Felipe Alou to block the position of first base for the 1972 season.

Nevertheless, Blomberg and Alou ended up each appearing in 95 games at the position in 1972, and the 23-year-old Blomberg easily outhit Alou. While his average dipped to .268, Blomberg hit 14 home runs in 299 at bats, slugging .488 in the process. He also continued to show the ability to not strike out—after 14 walks and 23 strikeouts in his 1971 campaign, he walked 38 times and struck out just 26 times. He would go on to walk more than he struck out—the walks were infrequent, but the whiffs were remarkably rare for a power hitter. He struck out just 140 times in 1,333 at bats—by contrast, contemporary slugger Dave Kingman struck out 122 times in 1973 alone—in just 305 at bats.

The 1973 season saw Blomberg come closest to realizing his seemingly unlimited potential. After hitting just .188 through April 29, he managed a 4-for-4 day to break out of his slump against Minnesota. He would not falter again for some time, getting most of the starts at designated hitter (Jim Ray Hart filled in for him some, due to nagging injuries), and Blomberg pushed his batting average above .400, earning the cover of *Sports Illustrated*, among others.

Blomberg topped .400 as late as June 28, but a summer-long slump eroded that mark to a still-great .329 average, with 12 home runs and just 25 strikeouts in 301 at bats. With Graig Nettles now manning third, Doc Medich holding down a rotation spot, and Sparky Lyle closing, the Yankees and Blomberg looked ready for the big time.

Though the Yankees got to the World Series by 1976 and won it in 1977, Blomberg was not a large part of the renaissance. His 1974 was nearly as good as his 1973—.311 average, 10 home runs in 264 at bats for a .475 slugging percentage, and just 33 strikeouts—but he suffered knee and shoulder injuries that limited him to just 106 at bats in 1975 and a mere 2 at bats in 1976.

Fully rehabilitated, Blomberg looked to resume his career in 1977, but a collision with an outfield wall (by then, Chris Chambliss, Carlos May, and Lou Piniella blocked the way at first base and DH) rendered Blomberg's 1977 a moot point.

After the 1977 season, he signed as a free agent with the Chicago White Sox. But the injuries had collectively sapped much of Blomberg's talent from him, and he managed just a .231 average in 156 at bats before calling it a career in the spring of 1979, when he failed to make the team out of spring training.

It is an exercise in futility to speculate on how good Blomberg, if healthy, might have been. Even with all that he suffered through, he ended with career marks of .293 batting average, .360 on-base percentage, and .473 slugging percentage. His 52 home runs in 1,333 at bats translates to 20 to 25 per season had he ever been fully healthy.

His stats are also undervalued by his era. Adjusted to a fairer hitter's experience by Baseball-Reference.com's neutralized stats, his career line is .316/.385/.507. (Just for comparison, Reggie Jackson's neutralized line is .277/.373/.517.)

Blomberg signed on in the spring of 2007 to manage the Bet Shemesh Blue Sox in the inaugural season of the Israeli Baseball League, which folded after one season. He deserved better—the Jewish Pete Reiser, with some better health, might have been one of the very best.

### 5. Phil Weintraub

*Bats Left, Throws Left*
*New York Giants, 1933–1935, 1937*
*Cincinnati Reds, 1937*
*Philadelphia Phillies, 1938*

*New York Giants, 1944–1945*

It is nearly impossible to understand how Phil Weintraub did not become a star first baseman in the major leagues. His statistical profile is one of a fine hitter, both superficially in the tools used to evaluate at the time (his career batting average was .295) and by the more exact measures we have today. His OPS+, which measures how his on-base percentage plus slugging measures against the league he played in, was 132 (100 is average). For contrast, Sammy Sosa's career OPS+ is 128.

After playing at Loyola College of Chicago, Weintraub joined the New York Giants in 1933. He received just 15 at bats for the world champions, as another left-handed, line-drive hitter, player/manager Bill Terry, manned first base.

The Giants let Weintraub go to Nashville of the Southern Association for more seasoning in 1934, and like Terry in 1930, Weintraub hit .401, the first man ever to top .400 in the league. He hit 16 home runs in just 371 at bats. He drove in 87 runs. He walked 68 times, struck out on just 36 occasions, and hit 3 home runs in a game. He was called up late in the season and hit .351 for the Giants.

*The Sporting News* said of Weintraub, December 13, 1934: "The Giants don't know what they're going to do with Phil."

The answer in 1935 was to bury him on the bench. Terry hit .341, while the offense provided by outfielders Mel Ott, Jo-Jo Moore, and Hank Lieber (all three 26 and younger) left few at bats for Weintraub. But Terry was 36 in 1935.

Surely Weintraub had to be the heir apparent!

Instead, Terry shipped Weintraub, along with pitcher Roy Parmalee, to St. Louis for middle infielder Burgess Whitehead. Injuries limited Terry in 1936, but the middling Sam Leslie, not Weintraub, was there to step in. Meanwhile, in St. Louis, a young man took over at first base named Johnny Mize. Cardinals general manager Branch Rickey soon saw that he had no need for Weintraub and parted with the thing he liked more than almost anything, a young player with unrealized potential, in exchange for the thing he liked even more, money.

Cincinnati kept him in the minors for the rest of 1936, even though he was hitting .371 in the International League with 80 RBI at the time of the deal. They made little use of him in 1937 as well. Les Scarsella and Buck Jordan were the no-names that prevented Weintraub from a full trial. He came full circle, returning to the Giants in July but getting just nine at bats for New York. Johnny McCarthy was the choice this time, even though the rate stats for his career-best season (.279/.322/.410) pale in comparison to Weintraub's season line, in 179 at bats, of .274/.348/.430.

Weintraub was promptly dumped by the Giants again, to the unaffiliated minor league club Baltimore. He was then purchased in June 1938 by the Phillies, who offered him a chance to play regularly for the first time in the major leagues. Weintraub did not disappoint, hitting .311 with a .422 on-base percentage in 351 at bats, and even collected the final hit in the Phils' old park, the Baker Bowl. The

Phillies promptly sold him to Boston at season's end.

While his rights were controlled by the Red Sox, Weintraub's chances of helping the major league club were remote at best. The incumbent, Jimmie Foxx, went out in 1939 and hit .360 with 35 home runs. Weintraub echoed Foxx's production with Minneapolis of the American Association, hitting .331 with 33 home runs in 1939. The next year was the same story: Foxx hit .297 with 36 home runs for the Sox; Weintraub hit .347 with 27 home runs for the Millers.

Then came the war. Foxx slowed down, but Weintraub continued slugging in the minors—he was well past 30 now. Foxx was replaced at first by Tony Lupien, who proved to be, well, no Jimmie Foxx. Weintraub's rights were shipped to the St. Louis Browns, then reacquired by, for a third time, the New York Giants.

As the league adopted "They're Either Too Young or Too Old" as the official theme song of Major League Baseball, the 36-year-old Weintraub showed he still had pop left in his bat. For the '44 Giants, he hit .316/.412/.524 in 361 at bats with 13 home runs. He followed that in 1945 with a .272/.389/.417 line, with another 10 home runs at age 37.

The 1946 Giants had five Jews. Weintraub was not one of them. The Giants had traded for Johnny Mize, and Weintraub's major league career was over.

How good was Weintraub? Terry, his manager, predecessor, and bête noire, finished with a .383 career on-base percentage and .492 slugging, for an OPS of .875. Weintraub's .400 on base plus .441 slugging is an .841 OPS. And of the two, on-base percentage is more valuable of an offensive tool.

Terry, by the way, is in the Hall of Fame. It isn't hard to imagine a different career path for Weintraub that would have included enshrinement as well.

### 6. Lou Limmer

*Bats Left, Throws Left*
*Philadelphia Athletics, 1951, 1954*

According to an April 5, 2007, obituary by the JTA (Jewish Telegraphic Agency), longtime minor league slugger Lou Limmer became the first Jewish baseball player ever to hold the office of president in his synagogue (in Limmer's case, Castle Hill Community Jewish Center in the Bronx).

This seems like it would be a natural career move, something akin to how caterpillars become butterflies. First basemen are, by nature, talkers. Current backup Boston first sacker Sean Casey is known as "the Mayor" for his gregariousness. There is a combination of political conversing and a search for information that takes place all at once between the person manning the position and the base runner.

Of the other Jewish first basemen, Hank Greenberg was certainly beloved enough to have become president of any congregation he desired (many fans, such as Alan Dershowitz, thought Greenberg would be the president of the United States). Greg Goossen has shown his abilities as an actor; surely congregation political leader wouldn't be beyond him. Even Ron Blomberg's talent at selling his autobiography would surely lend itself to the job.

That leaves aside the more obvious tactic, which would call for small-market teams, who cry poverty at a decibel level equal to synagogues on the High Holidays, to employ congregation presidents as first basemen. With most of them out of contention early in the season, what would they have to lose by sticking a lesser ballplayer into the bottom of the order, so that he might be able to kindly ask the passing base runners for financial relief? Whom better to target than baseball players, who by their very inclusion in the major leagues are guaranteed to be making well over $300,000 annually, with many surpassing that sum by millions of dollars?

Only the presence of uniforms that include identifying numbers, and often names, would prevent the most valued Jewish charity of all, the anonymous kind. Still, it is an idea whose time has come.

The A's, no stranger to financial woes, were 50-plus years ahead of their time by employing Lou Limmer, though they were likely persuaded more by his home run totals in the minor leagues (he hit 110 in his four seasons prior to his initial call-up in 1951, and a total of 244 in the minors, according to the Philadelphia A's Historical Society).

The Athletics, mired in decades of penny-pinching by owner/manager Connie Mack, had little talent on the field in 1951. Unfortunately for Limmer, most of that talent was at first base, in the person of Ferris Fain. While Limmer struggled to get at bats, Fain won batting titles in both 1951 and 1952, long after Limmer had been returned to the minor leagues. Limmer hit .159 with 5 home runs in 214 at bats, which wasn't going to strike job insecurity into the heart of any batting champion.

He did participate in a bit of Jewish baseball history, however, hitting a home run off the Detroit Tigers' Saul Rogovin, as Joe Ginsberg caught him on May 2, 1951. It was the first, and thus far only, Jewish battery and hitter in major league history.

Fain was eventually shipped out as the A's attempted to retool, and Limmer got his second and final shot in 1954. This time around, he hit .231, slugged 14 home runs (second on the team), and even managed the last home run in Philadelphia A's history. His long home runs during the pregame festivities even earned him the double-edged nickname "Babe Ruth of Batting Practice."

But attendance had fallen to just 304,666 for the season, less than half of what the crosstown Phillies drew. From that perspective, even Kansas City can seem like greener grass, so the A's took off, leaving Limmer behind in the minor leagues, this time for good.

It is hard to imagine a slugger the quality of Limmer languishing in the minors for his entire career in the era of the six-year minor league free agent and 30 teams. He won two minor league batting titles and finished in the top five of his league on seven different occasions. Had the Athletics used him as Castle Hill Community Jewish Center did, perhaps Philadelphia would have two teams still.

### 7. Greg Goossen

*Bats Right, Throws Right*
*New York Mets, 1965–1968*
*Seattle Pilots, 1969*
*Milwaukee Brewers, 1970*
*Washington Senators, 1970*

Goossen was, like Ed Kranepool, a young player who lost his prime development years playing for the early New York Mets. Those Mets were desperate for talent, so Goossen, Ron Swoboda, and many others who could have benefited from minor league time instead provided a sense of hope to fans as the Mets found 10th place each year.

Plucked away by the expansion Seattle Pilots in 1969, Goossen experienced a magical season, hitting .309 with 10 home runs in just 139 at bats for a .597 slugging percentage. But his magic did not travel with the franchise to Milwaukee, and after slumping to .255 and just .222 after being purchased midseason by the Senators, he never returned to the major leagues.

However, Goossen has found a postbaseball home acting in films, primarily as a stand-in for Gene Hackman. While it is hard to fashion an argument that Goossen made a huge difference for his oft-losing major league teams, is it possible that his presence was the difference in Hackman's finest films?

**Five Best Gene Hackman Movies with Greg Goossen**

*The Royal Tenenbaums*
*Unforgiven*
*The Birdcage*
*Get Shorty*
*The Firm*

**Five Best Gene Hackman Movies without Greg Goossen**

*The French Connection*
*Reds*
*Hoosiers*
*Superman*
*Crimson Tide*

**You be the judge. My vote is no.**

## 8. Jake Goodman

*Bats Unknown, Throws Unknown*
*Milwaukee Grays, 1878*
*Pittsburgh Alleghenys, 1882*

How can I fail to honor the memory of Jake Goodman, a Jewish first baseman who finished fifth in the National League in home runs in 1878? Well, the total that catapulted him to fifth was one home run. (When they call it the deadball era, they aren't complimenting the offenses.) He finished 7th in the league in strikeouts and 10th in total outs made.

The Grays weren't much better as a team, finishing at 15–45, though based on their runs scored and runs allowed, they should have been closer to 19–41. Like a guest too polite to make a host uncomfortable any longer, the Grays politely bowed and ceased to exist.

Goodman resurfaced with the 1882 Alleghenys of the American Association, forerunner to today's Pirates (Pittsburgh merged into the NL in 1887). There, Chappy Lane proved to be no contest for Goodman in the first base battle. Lane hit just .178 (and would be closed for renovations), while Goodman batted a robust .317, though his home run total dropped slightly, to zero. Nevertheless, Pittsburgh went with the younger Ed Smallwood in 1883, releasing Goodman and ending his major league career.

Little else is known about Goodman, who passed away in 1890. Records do not even indicate whether he batted lefty or righty. Still, as one of the earliest Jews in baseball history, he earns a place in this book. And one fortuitous afternoon in 1878 Milwaukee, he gave the city a thrill (his one home run) unrivaled until Laverne and Shirley went to work at the plant.

## 9. Mike Schemer
*Bats Left, Throws Left*
*New York Giants, 1945–1946*

Mike Schemer returned from World War II in time to play 1944 with Jersey City, a farm club of the New York Giants. By 1945 he was up with the big club as major league teams searched everywhere for able-bodied players.

Schemer acquitted himself nicely among the leftovers, hitting .333 in a part-time role (108 at bats). He served primarily as backup, incidentally, for Phil Weintraub. By 1946 he was only able to get a single at bat, with newly acquired Johnny Mize eating up the appearances at first base.

Schemer bounced around for a while after that, playing and managing with West Palm Beach in the Florida International League, pinch hitting for Sacramento of the Pacific Coast League. But like a lot of other players of that era, he lost his prime seasons to World War II.

### 10. Samuel Fishburn

*Bats Right, Throws Right*
*St. Louis Cardinals, 1919*

It is hard to imagine why Samuel Fishburn never got a chance to play—the Cardinals gave him just six at bats. He played one game at first, one at second for the Cardinals. But he was a shortstop by trade, having played 35 games for Reading of the International League before coming to the Cardinals.

The Cardinals had a light-hitting shortstop named Doc Lavan, while their first baseman, Dots Miller, hit even worse. But Fishburn couldn't get into the lineup.

In his one game at first, he made eight putouts without an error. At second base, three perfect chances. He had a single and a double in six times at the plate.

It was a small sample. But it certainly appears what Fishburn did was worthy of a second look.

| NAME | GAMES | AT BATS | OPS+ | WARP3 | Additional |
|---|---|---|---|---|---|
| 1. Hank Greenberg | 1394 | 5193 | 158 | 77.0 | 2-time AL MVP |
| 2. Mike Epstein | 907 | 2854 | 129 | 28.9 | 30 HR, 1969 |
| 3. Kevin Youkilis | 553 | 1922 | 119 | 27.1 | 2007 Gold Glove |
| 4. Ron Blomberg | 461 | 1333 | 140 | 15.0 | Hit .329 in 1973 |
| 5. Phil Weintraub | 444 | 1382 | 132 | 16.0 | |
| 6. Lou Limmer | 209 | 530 | 75 | 0.1 | 254 minor league HR |
| 7. Greg Goossen | 193 | 460 | 100 | 0.7 | |
| 8. Jake Goodman | 70 | 293 | 93 | 0.9 | |
| 9. Mike Schemer | 32 | 109 | 113 | 1.0 | |
| 10. Samuel Fishburn | 9 | 6 | 155 | 0.1 | 50 games at SS in minors |

**4**

# Second Base

In a 1976 *Esquire* magazine article naming an all-Jewish team, the number one Jewish second baseman was Hall of Famer Rod Carew. Indeed, the base hit machine finished with more than 3,000 hits, hit as high as .388 in a season, and earned a place in Adam Sandler's "Hanukkah Song."

Unfortunately, Carew isn't Jewish. He married a Jewish woman, but he did not convert. So much as we would like to claim him, he doesn't qualify, any more than my childhood friend David Lopez qualified for complaining to his mother about being served "*goyische* corned beef" in eighth grade. He (Carew, not Lopez) also, by career's end, played more at first base than second base, meaning that, had he converted, he'd merely be a backup to Mr. Greenberg in this book.

However, an excellent hitter, and a much better fielder than Carew, leads the all-Jewish team at second base:

*Buddy Myer*

Charles Solomon "Buddy" Myer. Though he finished with a .303 career batting average (Carew comes in at .328), their on-base percentages are nearly identical (.389 for Myer, .393 for Carew). The gap is wider than it would appear based on raw stats, for Myer played in the hit-happy 1930s; Carew began his career in the offensive 40-years-in-the-desert 1960s. Still, Myer is a fine choice for tops at second base.

A current second baseman, Ian Kinsler, is poised to challenge for supremacy at the keystone position. A messianic Jew, David Newhan, has had a productive career as well. Others, like Andy Cohen and Jimmie Reese, are more famous for having played for John McGraw or roomed with Babe Ruth, respectively. Ultimately, the lack of depth at the position suggests that much as baseball is losing some of its finest athletes to basketball and football today, many of the would-be Jewish double-play combos may have found themselves in the medical or legal professions instead.

## 1. Buddy Myer
*Bats Left, Throws Right*
*Washington Senators, 1925–1927*
*Boston Red Sox, 1928*
*Washington Senators, 1929–1941*
Buddy Myer is a mostly forgotten second baseman today. Yet his three top comparable players, according to Baseball-Reference.com, are Billy Herman, Arky Vaughan, and Joe Sewell, all three Hall of Famers. He leads all Jewish players

in hits and stolen bases, and is near the top in both batting average and on-base percentage.

It's not as if Myer played in relative obscurity—Washington, D.C., is a fairly high-profile city, being the nation's capital and all. And contrary to the popular memory of the Senators, Myer did not play for horrific teams. The Senators may be known for the phrase "First in war, first in peace, and last in the American League," and for coming out on the short end of lopsided trades (it can be argued that even in the Joe Hardy deal, they gave up too much), but in the years Myer was a regular for Washington, they finished fourth, fifth, second, third, third, first, seventh, sixth, third, sixth, and fifth. In other words, they were in the first division more often than not; in the third-place seasons, they won more than 90 games, but had the misfortune of playing in the same league as the Babe Ruth/Lou Gehrig Yankees and the Connie Mack second-dynasty Philadelphia Athletics.

Myer was a Mississippi product, born in Ellisville, and played at Mississippi A&M (now Mississippi State). After graduating in 1925, he made his debut with the Senators, after wowing the Southern Association sufficiently to earn the headline "Called 1925 Prize of Southern Loop" in the August 27, 1925, edition of *The Sporting News*. Though he received only eight at bats in the 1925 regular season, he sufficiently impressed his pennant-winning manager, Bucky Harris, to get eight more in the 1925 World Series.

He lived up to the expectations in 1926, batting .304 while handling shortstop for the Senators, though Washington slipped to fourth. Though he hit just 1 home run, he had 18 doubles and 6 triples. More importantly, he walked 45 times, to lift his on-base percentage to .370, and struck out on just 19 occasions. At age 22, his future seemed bright.

But Washington is an impatient town, and after just 51 at bats in the 1927 season for the Senators, when Myer hit a paltry .216, he was sent to the Boston Red Sox in exchange for journeyman middle infielder Topper Rigney. Myer hit about as he had in 1926 (and indeed, as he would for the remainder of his career), posting a .288 mark for the Sox, along with a .359 on-base percentage. His .281 season mark in batting average was buttressed by 56 walks, along with just 18 strikeouts—a more than 3-to-1 ratio.

Unlike many current Washington power brokers, Senators owner Clark Griffith was "willing to admit [his] mistakes," according to the December 20, 1928, edition of *The Sporting News*. The Senators traded five players to get back the one they'd dumped just 18 months earlier—and all five were major leaguers.

Griffith labeled the first Myer transaction "the dumbest deal I ever made," according to baseball historian Jack Kavanagh.

He would not regret the second deal. While each of the five players he dealt contributed at the big league level, Myer would easily outlast them all. He hit over .300 five of the next seven seasons, with solid-to-spectacular walk totals (he managed 102 free passes in 1934—an astounding number for a nonpower threat). His home run totals were meager (a season high of six), but he buttressed his singles with a fair amount of doubles and triples, reaching double figures in three-baggers seven times in his career.

Even as the Senators faltered, Myer didn't. In his age-34 season, he hit .336/.454/.465 for middling Washington, and even in his final season, though he hit a paltry .252 without power, he still managed a .360 on-base percentage in 107 at bats. Though war came to the country following that 1941 season, it is hard to imagine he'd have played any longer—his career totals were not impacted by Hitler.

The Hall of Fame (HOF) case for Myer is stronger if era isn't taken into account. His top three comparisons are in the Hall, it is true, but only Arky Vaughan is a good HOF selection—Herman and Sewell are both mistakes. Still, while he wouldn't be the best HOF inductee, he'd be far from the worst, and any team could win a championship with Buddy Myer at second base.

## 2. Ian Kinsler

*Bats Right, Throws Right*
*Texas Rangers, 2006–*

This is a glory time for Jewish infielders. Between Kevin Youkilis at first base, Ian Kinsler at second, and Ryan Braun at third, it can be argued that no other era has had as many elite Jewish players around the horn. What's more, with all of them shy of 30, the era is likely to continue.

However, of the three, Kinsler is the player most likely to conclude his career at the top of the Jewish rankings. While Youkilis is a skilled hitter and fielder, he will be hard-pressed to overtake the all-time great Hank Greenberg. Ryan Braun's fielding difficulties sent him to left field in 2008.

But while Kinsler is a very different player than Buddy Myer, he has already displayed abilities that could surpass Myer's if he has a long career—and judging by Texas's attempts to lock him up to a long-term deal, the Rangers see such a possibility as increasingly likely. In February 2008, Texas signed Kinsler to a five-year, $22 million contract with a sixth-year club option, this despite the fact that Kinsler was in Texas's control for another four years. Kinsler rewarded Texas with a 2008 season line of .319/.375/.517 before a sports hernia prematurely ended his season in August.

Kinsler was not highly regarded out of high school; a 29th-round pick, he chose not to sign with the Diamondbacks, and the Texas Rangers took him in the 17th round of the 2003 draft. But his first full professional season in 2004 put him on the prospect map. He hit .401 with a .687 slugging percentage in A-ball, followed that with a .300/.400/.480 line in his first exposure to AA, and by 2005 was named the eighth best prospect in all of baseball by *Baseball America*.

The Rangers then converted him from shortstop to second base, not because of his own defensive shortcomings, but due to the impending free agency of Alfonso Soriano. He hit .274 with 23 home runs at AAA, and the Rangers dealt Soriano so Kinsler could have the second base job.

Whether Kinsler is considered merely a very good player or a near superstar depends on how one ranks his defense. His offensive contributions cannot be questioned. In his rookie year, he put up a line of .286/.347/.454 and followed in 2007 with .263/.355/.441. That OPS total ranked him 10th among second basemen in 2006, 12th in 2007. And he put those numbers up while battling a number of injuries—he dislocated his left thumb in 2006, missed a month with a foot injury in 2007, and had the hernia in 2008. Otherwise, his counting stats—52 home runs through three seasons— would be even more impressive.

Defensively, Kinsler shows both his background as a shortstop and the recent conversion to second base within his performance. His range is unquestioned—he consistently gets to far more balls than Derek Jeter, and he led the major league in range factor in 2007. However, the by-product of his range has been to lead the major leagues in errors by a second baseman in both 2006 and 2007. Of course, errors are a lousy way to evaluate defense (if Player A gets to 100 more balls than Player B, but makes errors on 10 of them, he's still made 90 additional plays than Player B)—Kinsler's 34 errors in his first two full seasons equal the total over that same span by Bill Mazeroski, widely considered the finest defender ever at the keystone position.

Ultimately, I'd sooner take the chance that a wide-ranging defensive player will make more plays as he matures than that a player will start getting to more balls. And from seeing Kinsler play, there's little doubt in my mind that he will convert more of those plays in the coming years. Add plus defense to his offensive totals, and he needn't improve to make a claim as greatest Jewish second baseman—he merely needs longevity.

Kinsler, a friendly and approachable player, would be proud to hold the title. While his mother is Catholic, his father is Jewish, and according to Kinsler, one conversion had already taken place—his father, who grew up in the Bronx as a Yankees fan, is now steadfastly for the Rangers.

### 3. Sammy Bohne

*Bats Right, Throws Right*
*St. Louis Cardinals, 1916*
*Cincinnati Reds, 1921–1926*
*Brooklyn Dodgers, 1926*

Sammy Bohne was certainly a fighter. His performance on the San Francisco sandlots earned him a shot with the Cardinals at the age of 19, making him the youngest player in the league.

He resurfaced five years later with Cincinnati and laid claim on the second base job, putting together a fine rookie year, hitting .285/.347/.398, which was an above-average OPS+ in 1924, and added, by reports, a plus glove to go with it. He was in the National League top 10 in walks, runs, triples, and stolen bases—though the steals were negated some by his league lead in caught stealing.

But Bohne never lived up to his 1921 season—it would prove to be his high-water mark in virtually every category. He slipped to .274/.344/.360 in 1922 and in 1923 fell to .252/.316/.340. By 1924 he'd lost the starting keystone spot to Hughie Critz.

But Bohne did score an important victory during that time. According to baseball historian Norman L. Macht, a journalist accused Bohne and a teammate of throwing games. Not only did Bohne deny the claim, he sued for libel and won—an awfully high legal threshold to cross. Such accusations were common following the Black Sox scandal of 1919; such victories by players accused were far rarer.

Macht also points out that Bohne broke up a no-hit bid by Dazzy Vance with two outs in the ninth on June 17, 1923. Clearly, the man had plenty of fight in him.

Bohne went on to play with Vance late in the 1926 season, after Brooklyn purchased him on June 15. But he hit just .201 in 1926 and headed to Minneapolis, where, like Andy Cohen a few years later, he played second base for the Millers. He hit .271 with 11 homers in 1927, .294 with a pair of long balls in 1928. By 1929 Bohne was a .241 hitter and a player/coach.

But that season, he got perhaps his biggest hit. During a Fourth of July brawl between the Millers and the neighboring St. Paul Saints, Bohne's role in the fight earned him the *Minneapolis Journal* headline "Sammy Bohne Doesn't Play, but Gets More Hits Than Those That Do."

## 4. David Newhan

*Bats Left, Throws Right*
*San Diego Padres, 1999–2000*
*Philadelphia Phillies, 2000–2001*
*Baltimore Orioles, 2004–2006*
*New York Mets, 2007*
*Houston Astros, 2008*

While David Newhan is not on a Hall of Fame career path, it is unlikely that any Jewish player has had a better month than Newhan's first after signing with the Orioles in June 2004. And to be sure, such a performance was unexpected—Newhan has Hall of Fame bloodlines, but they stem from the J. G. Taylor Spink wing of the Hall, where baseball writers are honored.

Newhan was born and raised in California, getting the chance to experience the major leagues as he grew up. His father, Ross Newhan, was the esteemed baseball writer for the *Los Angeles Times* from 1967 to 2004. So Newhan received batting tips from Rod Carew while finding time to get bar mitzvahed at his Conservative synagogue.

Newhan became a sought-after player, recruited out of Cypress College to play at Georgia Tech for a season. He manned first base for a Yellow Jackets team that included shortstop Nomar Garciaparra, catcher Jason Varitek, and probably the best of the bunch, center fielder Jay Payton. But Tech coach Jim Morris had promised Newhan the second base job, so he transferred to Pepperdine University after one season. There, he played left field, winning All-

Conference honors and preparing for a life as a major league utility player, though he didn't know it yet.

The Athletics drafted Newhan in the 17th round, just like Ian Kinsler, but unlike Kinsler, a breakout offensive performance did not translate to organizational respect. Newhan converted to second base at the request of his A-ball manager, then proceeded to outhit his double-play partner, future star Miguel Tejada. He hit .301 with a .538 slugging percentage—Oakland yawned, and Newhan repeated single-A. After three years with the A's, Newhan was dealt to San Diego, where he was finally able to advance, making his major league debut in 1999.

But Newhan's ability to hit in the minor leagues betrayed him at the big league level. He hit .140 in 1999, and despite a strong spring landing him San Diego's second base job in 2000, he was demoted after 37 at bats with a .162 average. He was dealt to the Phillies—his slump continued. His path then further diverged from success when he injured his arm slamming into an outfield wall. Newhan missed the 2002 season, and any major league success became extremely unlikely. He was 29 entering the 2003 season, long past the sell-by date for prospects.

Despite Newhan's strong 2003 performance, hitting .348 for AAA Colorado Springs, and a .328/.389/.557 line for AAA Oklahoma in 2004, he did not get a call-up by either the Rockies or the Rangers. On June 18, 2004, he asked for his release and signed with the Baltimore Orioles, who had a roster need. What followed was extraordinary.

Newhan got his first major league at bat in three years that night, as a pinch hitter. He crushed a 435-foot home run. Over his next 33 games, Newhan hit .403 with a .447 on-base percentage. He had three four-hit games. In his first 44 games played with the Orioles, he managed to go hitless just three times. And he managed his hitting groove while constantly shifting positions—for the season, he played 32 games at DH, 24 in right field, 19 in left field, 17 at third base, and 2 at first base. Notably, he didn't play any games at second base, his most comfortable position.

He finished 2004 with a .311/.361/.453 line, along with 11 stolen bases. The Orioles thought they had a building block for their future.

But in recent years, if the Orioles have believed something, much money could be made by betting on the opposite. Newhan came crashing back to earth in 2005, hitting .202/.279/.312. He split time between the Orioles and AAA in 2006, the Mets and AAA in 2007. Both seasons, he struggled in the majors (.252 and .203 batting average), while excelling in the minors—putting up a .347/.413/.572 line with AAA New Orleans in 2007, in a pitcher's home park.

He signed with the Houston Astros for 2008, where he played mostly second base. Of course, one can never be sure with Newhan's unconventional career path what to expect next.

## 5. Andy Cohen
*Bats Right, Throws Right*
*New York Giants, 1926, 1928–1929*

Before Hank Greenberg became the definitive Jewish-American baseball icon, Andrew Howard Cohen was widely expected to be that man. And Cohen, geographically, made more sense—while Greenberg played in Detroit, a hotbed of anti-Semitism, Cohen played in New York, the Jewish capital of the United States.

Amazingly, there has never been a huge Jewish star in New York, despite a large number of Jewish players. One can only imagine the media and popular swarm such a star would receive; indeed, the reception for Cohen upon arrival in New York provides a glimpse into it.

Cohen was not, however, a New Yorker by birth. He and his younger brother, Syd, who went on to pitch in the big leagues as well, grew up in El Paso, Texas, and both attended the University of Alabama. The elder Cohen was a multisport star at Alabama, helping the Crimson Tide on the baseball diamond, the basketball court, and (of course) the football field.

Again worth noting—while many Jews point to Hank Greenberg's success as a key in combating the stereotype that Jews aren't athletic, Greenberg was far from an athlete in the well-rounded sense; his lumbering gait made him arguably the slowest runner in the league for most of his career. Cohen's all-around abilities might have helped defeat this idea in a more comprehensive sense.

When Cohen finished in Alabama, he quickly signed with Waco of the Texas League, and it wasn't long before he drew the attention of major league scouts, hitting .319 as a

20-year-old. According to *The Sporting News*, Giants manager John McGraw purchased Cohen, intending to bring him to New York in time for the 1927 season, but he was so impressed, he convinced Waco to let Cohen play some for New York in 1926, in exchange for the sum of $25,000.

"The young Hebrew, Andy Cohen, was allowed to play second base—his first appearance in a National League game—and he surely looked and acted like the real article," *The Sporting News* wrote in its June 10, 1926, edition.

How big was Cohen's debut? A week later, *The Sporting News* made Cohen its featured ballplayer on page 1.

"*Oi gevald!*" screamed the lead on June 17, 1926. "John McGraw has that Jewish baseball player he's been looking for these many years. At least, he thinks he has. The leader of the Giants, at this time, is not so sure what he's going to do with him, but the fact remains that the Jewish boy is in captivity and that's something when it is considered Israel's children are the real dodos of the baseball woods." Thanks, *Sporting News*! Most of us were a generation removed from European pogroms . . . but thanks!

It gets better. "He is five feet eight, weighs 155 pounds, and has all the natural characteristics (physically) of his race—thick, dark hair, dark skin and keen mentality." Just like the dodo.

The 21-year-old Cohen hit .257 in 35 at bats, failing to unseat the incumbent Frankie Frisch, the Fordham Flash. The Giants then traded one Hall of Fame second baseman for another, dealing Frisch for Rogers Hornsby, and Cohen was farmed out to Buffalo for more seasoning.

By the middle of June 1927, it was clear that Cohen had nothing left to prove at the minor league level.

"Infielder Andy Cohen is showing high class ability in all departments of his game, his fielding being of sensational order, and his hitting of high proportions," *The Sporting News* wrote on June 2, 1927. "His swatting mark recently stood at .431, which placed him at the top of the league in stickwork." He finished the season at .355.

How highly regarded was Cohen at this point? The Giants dealt away Hornsby, after he hit .361/.448/.586, with 26 home runs and 125 RBI, to give Cohen a clean shot at the second base job. McGraw may have wanted Cohen for box office appeal, but no one wanted to win more than John McGraw. Clearly, he believed Cohen was the real deal.

And so did *The Sporting News*, with the April 19, 1928, headline "Gotham's Gone Wild over Andrew Cohen." The subheads are even better: "Work in First Week Establishes Youngster as a Star," and "New York Club Provides a Suite in Hotel for Him That He May Meet Mobs of Worshippers."

Detailing the largest ovation in Giants history, when Cohen was literally carried off the field after notching two hits on opening day, *The Sporting News* went on to note, "Stories of the kid's life were hurried into the metropolitan newspapers and his picture was flashed before enthusiastic crowds in the movie theaters."

In other words, even then, New York prospects were overhyped. Cohen did not live up to the clippings or adoration of that first week. By August, McGraw had moved Cohen down to the seventh spot in the batting order, and Cohen lost some playing time to Randy Reese down the stretch. The Giants fell two games short of the pennant.

Overall, Cohen had a decent first full season—he hit .274/.318/.403 with 9 home runs at age 23. But in a time of offensive explosion, such numbers were not particularly distinguished—his offensive contributions ranked eighth in his own lineup.

As for attendance? Considering that in both the 1927 and 1928 seasons, the Giants finished with nearly identical records, both times finished two games out of first place, and that the only difference in the lineup was the presence of Hornsby in '27 and Cohen in '28, it would be fair to compare the two. In 1927 attendance was 858,190. In 1928 it was 916,191, a nearly 7 percent increase.

Despite Cohen's middling 1928, the *New Yorker* took notice of the young second baseman with a "Talk of the Town" profile. Not only did Cohen receive "more presents this season than any other player," but Cohen "likes to make talks before boys' clubs. He reads both Will Durant and Edgar Guest, and goes to most of the musical comedies." And the magazine noted proudly, "His secret ambition is to go back and get his degree."

The 1929 season held not only the stock market crash, but also the collapse of the Andy Cohen worshipping market.

Cohen got the majority of the playing time at second base, but Randy Reese got plenty as well—Cohen's at bats dropped from 504 to 347. His overall numbers were a pedestrian .294/.319/.383, and he failed to provide much speed on the base paths, swiping just three bases.

Cohen's major league time was over. As my great-grandfather did, Cohen made his way to Newark, playing second base for the Bears alongside fellow New York castoff Wally Pipp. But while Great-Grandpa stayed and built a world-class bakery, Cohen headed to Minneapolis, where he played world-class second base for the Millers of the American Association.

Thanks to Stew Thornley, who wrote the definitive Minneapolis Millers book, we know that Cohen played for a number of championship teams in Minneapolis, posting high batting averages and decent power numbers each year. Considering the high level of the AA, and that Cohen's career in the majors was snuffed out before he reached his prime, it is fair to posit that Cohen might have carved out a solid career in the bigs, with just one more chance. His 1937 campaign, .320, 11 homers, 82 RBI at second base, was not the mark of a man who couldn't hit big league pitching. For comparison, Phil Weintraub, in 1939, hit .331 for Minneapolis. And a pretty fair hitter, Ted Williams, hit .366 for the 1938 Millers.

Cohen retired after the 1939 season, becoming a wandering minor league manager and sometime major league coach. He won league titles with both the Eau Claire Bears of the Northern League and the Denver Bears of the Western League, showing himself to be both an effective manager and an arctophile.

Cohen's moment of managerial glory came early in the 1960 season. Eddie Sawyer, who managed the Phils through consecutive last-place seasons in 1958 and 1959, abruptly quit after opening day of the 1960 season. Cohen took over for Sawyer on April 14, 1960, and saw his starter, Curt Simmons, get knocked out in the second inning. But after one reliever, Ruben Gomez, held down the Milwaukee Braves for three innings, Don Cardwell followed and earned a six-inning victory, even homering in his own cause. The Phils won the home opener, 5–4, in 10 innings and quickly replaced Cohen with Gene Mauch. Did replacing an undefeated manager lead directly to the Phils' 1964 collapse just four years later, when the team blew a 6½ game lead with 12 games left? I'll leave that to you.

Cohen returned to his native El Paso and built from scratch the University of Texas El Paso (UTEP) baseball program, with some help from his brother, Syd. The UTEP field has the unlikely name of Cohen Stadium in honor of the two men.

Still, Cohen's entire life in baseball has the feel of someone who came upon the edge of the spotlight, only to back away from it. El Paso may know Andy Cohen's name, but with the right break along the way, Cohen might have been nearly as famous a baseball surname as Greenberg.

*Well nothing like that happened, but what do you suppose?*
*Why little Andy Cohen socked the ball upon the nose*
*Then from the stands and bleachers the fans in*
*    triumph roared,*
*And Andy raced to second and the other runner scored*
*Soon they took him home in triumph amidst the blare*
*    of auto honks,*
*There may be no joy in Mudville, but there's plenty*
*    in The Bronx.*

FROM "COHEN AT THE BAT," AUTHOR UNKNOWN, REPRINTED
IN *American Hebrew*, APRIL 23, 1948

## 6. Jimmie Reese

*New York Yankees, 1930–1931*
*St. Louis Cardinals, 1932*

You know the phrase "a baseball lifer"? Jimmie Reese is a
baseball lifer. He was a bat boy for Lefty O'Doul and hit
fungoes for Garret Anderson. He roomed with Babe Ruth
and was honorary captain of an American League All-Star
team that faced Barry Bonds. He signed his first professional baseball contract when Joe DiMaggio was 12 and was
still coaching after Nolan Ryan retired.

Whatever he did clearly worked, as he was still hitting
fungoes with deadly accuracy into his 90s. Reese grew up
Hymie Solomon, and changed his name, as many Jews did,
to avoid anti-Semitism. The decision worked out well—in
a charity game, catcher Ike Danning and pitcher Harry

Ruby, the brilliant songwriter who penned "Hooray for Captain Spaulding" for Groucho Marx, decided to forgo signs and communicate in Yiddish. Reese, the covert Jew, went 4-for-4.

Reese had a long minor league career sandwiched around parts of three major league seasons. At age 28, he hit .346 for the New York Yankees—his roommate, Ruth, hit .359. While 1930 was one of the best offensive years in baseball history (the American League hit .288, the National League .303), .346 is still .346.

Reese's hitting tailed off in 1931, with a .241 average, and he followed with a .265 average in St. Louis in 1932. It seems as if there were only two eras Reese's glove wouldn't have kept him in the major leagues at second base—the late '20s/early '30 and the late '90s into today.

But his work in the Pacific Coast League, a top-flight minor league, cannot be questioned. He earned raves for his glove work, with Dennis Snelling calling Reese "arguably the greatest fielding second baseman in Coast League history" in his definitive statistical history of the league. But Reese hit plenty, notching a .337 batting average in 1929 for the Oakland Oaks, and hitting .331 and .311 in his first two years back from the majors, 1933–1934, for the Los Angeles Angels. He finished with 1,809 hits in the PCL, a legacy unto itself.

Reese was just getting started, becoming a coach in Seattle, San Diego, even Hawaii. From 1972 until his death in 1994, he was the conditioning coach for the Angels. Nolan

Ryan even named a son after him, and his number 50 was retired by the team.

According to his *New York Times* obit, he had no survivors. But that seems narrow—baseball was his family, and Reese's legacy is all over the game.

## 7. Jake Pitler
*Bats Right, Throws Right*
*Pittsburgh Pirates, 1917–1918*

World War I stands unequivocally as a regrettable human tragedy. But for Jake Pitler, the resulting man shortage within major league baseball provided an opportunity. The 5'8" second baseman got his chance at the big leagues, when at age 23, the Pirates tabbed him to man second base.

Once he got to the show, Pitler could have been forgiven for thinking he was still in the bushes. The 1917 Pirates were a terrible, terrible team. The Pirates hit .238 as a team. Their team on-base percentage was .293, and the team slugging percentage was .298. I mean, it was the deadball era, but still, these marks were awful. They were last or next to last in the league in nearly every vital offensive category— they scored 464 runs, or almost 3 runs per game exactly.

So just 192,807 fans turned out to see Jake Pitler's one season in the spotlight—all but one of his major league at bats came during the 1917 season. Essentially, Pitler in 1917 *was* the Pirates. The team's line was .238/.293/.298; Pitler's was .233/.297/.280. It is safe to assume that Pitler had responsibility for a lot of ground balls on the right side of the infield—the regular first baseman was Honus Wagner, who was, after all, 43 years old. Hard to imagine the Dutchman calling off 23-year-old Pitler very often.

When the war ended, Pitler's limitations as a 23-year-old in A-ball asserted themselves. He played in the minor leagues for another 15 years, with much of that time coming in the New York–Penn League. That made him a natural candidate to manage in the circuit, and he piloted teams in Elmira, Scranton, and even Wilkes-Barre.

Pitler went on to a long career in coaching with the Dodgers, managing their Pony League teams to back-to-back titles in 1939–1940, and coached at the big league level from 1947 to 1957. Rather than follow the team to Los Angeles, he stayed in the Northeast as a scout. His reputation was built on observations such as recognizing that Gil Hodges was a star-in-the-making, though it is safe to assume that Branch Rickey probably knew that already.

Ultimately, evaluating a player like Pitler is extremely difficult, with so much of his prime played in semiorganized circuits. But unlike the 1917 Pittsburgh Pirates, Pitler was honored twice by the Brooklyn Dodgers. It is possible that the only one more upset about the Dodgers leaving Brooklyn than the citizens of Flatbush was Pitler himself.

### 8. Jake Atz

*Bats Right, Throws Right*
*Washington Senators, 1902*
*Chicago White Sox, 1907–1909*

One of my favorite stories of the Jewish people who changed their names is Jake Atz, longtime minor league player and renowned minor league manager. Atz apparently changed his name from John Zimmerman, which is certainly not the least Jewish name, but far from the most Semitic . . . to Jake Atz? Really? This is how we're passing? When a Jewish mother hears "Jake Atz," she doesn't think "I wonder if he's Jewish." She thinks, "He sounds perfect for my Ruthie! I wonder what minor league players make."

He got a brief trial with the Senators in 1902, in the city where he was born. Most of his 20s was spent trying to make good in minor league towns from Albany to Troy, New York, with a dose of Portland, Oregon, mixed in.

The White Sox purchased Atz in 1907 and gave him a chance to supplant George Davis. This was no easy task—the in-prime Davis, a Hall of Famer, would have easily beaten back Atz's challenge. But Davis was 37, and his average slipped to just .216 in 1908. Atz hit .194, but with his relative youth and batting eye (he supplemented that .194 with enough walks to lift his on-base percentage to .311), he beat out Davis for the keystone job on the 1909 White Sox.

Atz put up a .236/.309/.299 line in 1909, which was far from awful, considering the times. The American League hit just .244 in 1909. The White Sox, as a team, pitched to a 2.05 ERA. That was second in the American League.

Chicago jettisoned Atz in 1910 (maybe they found out he was Jewish?) for Rollie Zeider, but the Sox didn't solve their second base problem until they acquired Hall of

Famer Eddie Collins in 1915. By then, Atz was well into his managing career, which was far more distinguished than his time on the field. Atz won seven consecutive titles with Fort Worth of the Texas League during the 1920s, five times topping 100 victories. Such a performance hasn't been matched at any level, and his lifetime 1,972 wins as a skipper is 12th all time for minor league managers.

It is reasonable to argue that Atz had a better major league tenure than Pitler. But ultimately, Pitler's long minor league career—a 15-year edge in playing career—must be taken into account.

### 9. Heinie Scheer
*Bats Right, Throws Right*
*Philadelphia Athletics, 1922–1923*
You can normally count me among those who cast a wary eye upon nostalgia. The world is a more interesting place with the Internet. I enjoy the convenience of cell phones. And on the whole, life is much easier for us without dinosaurs. But is it really a better world without as many baseball players named Heinie?

The facts are inarguable. Major League Baseball has 22 Heinies in its illustrious history. But the Heinie phenomenon is a pre-Eisenhower one: none of the 22 Heinies played after World War II.

Heinie Scheer made his way to the major leagues early, earning a spot with the Philadelphia Athletics in 1922 at age 21. But while the A's were powerhouses in 1912, and later in

1932, the 1922 vintage finished just 65–89. Scheer hit .170, but it wasn't an empty .170—he added 4 home runs. Still, he hit .170. The A's brought in Jimmy Dykes, who shared the job with Scheer. The two played to a near draw—Dykes, 26, hit .252/.318/.353, while Scheer, just 22, hit .238/.301/.314.

But then the A's were presented with an opportunity they couldn't pass up. Scheer was at the center of a trade with Milwaukee of the American Association. In exchange for Scheer, outfielder Wid Matthews, and $40,000, Connie Mack acquired Al Simmons.

Scheer went on to a solid career as a minor league second baseman, even forming a Jewish double-play combination with Moe Berg when the latter still played shortstop with the 1926 Reading Keystones of the International League.

As for Simmons? He finished with 2,927 hits, a career line of .334/.380/.535, and had three seasons with more than 150 RBI. Six different seasons, he finished in the top 10 of MVP voting. It was viewed as one of the finest trades in Philadelphia Athletics history.

One wonders, though, if Connie Mack, in retrospect, might have been better off holding on to Heinie. After all, they have become quite scarce.

## 10. Al Federoff
*Bats Right, Throws Right*
*Detroit Tigers, 1951–1952*
A good-field, no-hit second baseman, and yet another Jewish player at the position who went on to manage, Al Federoff

got ample time to improve his hitting prior to coming to Detroit. He played for Jamestown in the New York–Penn League but failed to distinguish himself with the bat. He combined bat and glove with Flint of the Class B Interstate League in 1948, batting .291 with a .367 on-base percentage, and leading the circuit in stolen bases with 22. But this failed to convince many in baseball of his ability to hit in the majors.

When incumbent second baseman Jerry Priddy broke his leg early in the 1952 season, the Tigers, running last in the American League, summoned Federoff to hold down the position. To give a sense of the lack of confidence even the Tigers had in Federoff, listen to manager Fred Hutchinson, as quoted by the July 30, 1952, *Sporting News:* "We know from what we saw at Lakeland that the guy can make the plays," Hutchinson said. "His hitting picked up at Buffalo and he may be ready for the big leagues now. Anyway, he's our second baseman." Can you feel the enthusiasm?

Senators manager Bucky Harris added his thoughts in the same article: "Sure, he's a frail-looking guy, but that isn't necessarily a handicap." Where was Federoff's Jewish mother?

Federoff himself said, "This is the best chance I ever had. They're letting me play regularly, and if I don't make good I'll have no one to blame but myself." Unfortunately, he didn't make good, hitting just .242/.294/.277, paltry numbers for even a middle infielder in the early '50s. He never played major league ball again. But the Tigers employed him as a manager for a decade from 1960 to 1969, and he delivered a pair of league titles.

By 2008 he was impressing with his personality far beyond the limited accolades he'd received as a player.

"I sat next to Mr. Federoff at Comerica Park for Opening Day 2008," an anonymous "DetroitTigersFan" said of Federoff on his Baseball-Reference.com page. "His knowledge of the game is surpassed only by his class. A true gem."

### 11. Lou Rosenberg
*Bats Right, Throws Right*
*Chicago White Sox, 1923*

Lou Rosenberg was the second-youngest player in the American League when he received his four at bats for the 1923 Chicago White Sox. But reaching the majors that young was not always a blessing, as a poor trial often landed players back in the obscurity of the minors. And with so many minor leagues, so few major league jobs, a player was often better off getting his chance when he was at his peak—a second opportunity, far more often than not, wasn't forthcoming.

The names on the 1923 AL list of youngest players is littered with players who never saw big league action again. Of the 10 most youthful on the junior circuit, only two players saw action in more than three subsequent seasons. One, George Grant, pitched in 8²/₃ innings in 1923 for the Browns, posting a subpar 5.19 ERA (19 percent below league average), but the Browns being the Browns, he pitched another two below-average seasons in St. Louis before being shipped to the Cleveland Indians, where he turned the trick four more times. In other words, even with his relative longevity, it is hard to call Grant a success.

The same cannot be said for the 10th man on the list: Lou Gehrig. Of course, even at age 20, Gehrig made the most of his 26 at bats, hitting .423/.464/.769.

So it is distinctly possible that despite ample ability, Lou Rosenberg never got the chance to show it. But with the White Sox starting Hall of Famer Eddie Collins, Rosenberg would have had to be Gehrig to have gotten that chance.

| NAME | GAMES | AT BATS | OPS+ | WARP3 | Additional |
|---|---|---|---|---|---|
| 1. Buddy Myer | 1923 | 7038 | 108 | 75.8 | 2,131 hits |
| 2. Ian Kinsler | 371 | 1424 | 117 | 22.6 | |
| 3. Sammy Bohne | 663 | 2315 | 81 | 13.9 | |
| 4. David Newhan | 413 | 986 | 81 | 3.1 | |
| 5. Andy Cohen | 262 | 886 | 80 | 5.1 | 2,178 minor league hits |
| 6. Jimmie Reese | 232 | 742 | 84 | 4.2 | |
| 7. Jake Pitler | 111 | 383 | 75 | 2.0 | 23-year minor leaguer |
| 8. Jake Atz | 209 | 605 | 83 | 3.6 | |
| 9. Heinie Scheer | 120 | 345 | 45 | 0.5 | |
| 10. Al Federoff | 76 | 235 | 56 | −0.1 | |
| 11. Lou Rosenberg | 3 | 4 | 32 | −0.1 | |

# 5

## Third Base

⚾

**T**hird base is a paradox for the Jewish people. Given the lack of Jewish players at the position, you'd think the bag was made of pork. Just nine Jewish major leaguers have played primarily third base, and of those nine, just two have played more than one major league season. It hasn't been for lack of opportunity—overwhelmingly, the Jewish third basemen have played for poor teams, and any hint of talent would have allowed them to secure a permanent place. Even Ryan Braun, a supremely talented hitter and the 2007 National League Rookie of the Year, played third base so poorly that the Brewers immediately shifted him to the outfield.

Then there is the finest Jewish third baseman, Al Rosen. Rosen had a prime as impressive as any third baseman in major league history. But an established player

*Al Rosen*

blocked his path until age 26, and back injuries ended his productivity by his early 30s. Something cosmic appears to be at work here.

## 1. Al Rosen
*Bats Right, Throws Right*
*Cleveland Indians, 1947–1956*

Though it is easy to criticize Cleveland's decision to keep Al Rosen from regular action until he was 26 years old, in retrospect it couldn't have been an easy decision to make, even when they did it in 1950. Ken Keltner was enormously popular in Cleveland and had manned third since 1938, when he hit 26 home runs as a 21-year-old. Even in 1948, Keltner had put up his finest offensive season, hitting .297/.395/.522 for the last Cleveland World Championship team. And Keltner's defensive reputation was stellar—back in 1941, his defensive plays helped to end Joe DiMaggio's 56-game hitting streak.

But had Cleveland truly known what they had in Rosen, they might have cut bait sooner anyway. Rosen led the American League in home runs in his first full season with 37, and walked 100 times to boot, putting up a .287/.405/.543 line for the Indians. He continued his strong play in 1951–1952, while Cleveland struggled in an American League with the Yankees, but no wild card, finishing second both seasons.

The script was similar in 1953. This time, Rosen put up the best season any third baseman has ever had. Rosen's line was .336/.422/.613. He hit 43 home runs and knocked in 145 runs. He missed the Triple Crown by .001 (Mickey Vernon of the Senators hit .337), and when word of Rosen's final tally made it to Washington, the Senators supposedly got out intentionally to get their teammate the batting title. Regardless, Rosen was voted the Most Valuable Player unanimously.

By the measure of OPS+, Al Rosen had the finest offensive season of any third baseman ever in 1953. His OPS+ was 179 (100 is average), meaning it was 79 percent better than average. By contrast, Alex Rodriguez's 2007, when he hit .314 with 54 home runs and 156 RBI, produced an OPS+ of 177.

In 1954 Rosen hit .300/.404/.503 for an Indians team that won 111 games, though the Giants upset them in the World Series. Still, Rosen missed time, playing in just 137 games, after missing a total of 6 games over the previous four seasons. Back and leg problems had begun to sap Rosen of what should have been the second half of a Hall of Fame career. Rosen had a pair of seasons that were productive, but they fit better in Ken Keltner's career than Rosen's. After 1956, Rosen retired, at the age of 32. He was robbed, and so were Jewish fans. He had a long career as a baseball executive, but he should have had a place in Cooperstown.

## 2. Cy Block
*Bats Right, Throws Right*
*Chicago Cubs, 1942, 1945–1946*
In the 1940s, the Chicago Cubs organization collected high-

average, low-power, single-syllable third basemen. Starting at the hot corner was Stan Hack, a legitimate star player who hit .301, but he never managed more than eight home runs in a season.

Hack blocked the way for Cy Block, an eerily similar player.

Block debuted at age 19 with the D-level Paragould Rebels of the Northeast Arkansas League, hitting .323 with 7 home runs. As he climbed the minor league ladder, he continued to hit over .300, while reaching the high single digits in homers—Block's minor league seasons would fit perfectly within Hack's career.

But while the man blocking Al Rosen slowed down at age 33, Hack continued producing right through World War II and into 1947. Block got scattered at bats in 1942 and again after returning from service in 1945–1946. He hit remarkably well in 1942, poorly in 1945–1946, though in each case, in far too few at bats to conclude anything from his performance. His career major league line of .302/.383/.358 in 53 at bats is even Hackesque.

Block actually split time in '45 and '46 between the Cubs and Nashville of the Southern Association, where he hit .354 and .360. He finished his career in Buffalo of the International League, with the average dropping each season. He hit a combined .276 for Buffalo in 845 at bats over three seasons; Stan Hack hit .273 in his final year.

There but for the grace of Stan Hack went Cy Block—the

Stan Hack doppelgänger. And as the noted baseball writer Bill Mazer told me when I was a guest on his radio program, "It didn't help that the Cubs manager, Charlie Grimm, didn't share Cy's religion."

### 3. Mickey Rutner

*Bats Right, Throws Right*
*Philadelphia Athletics, 1947*

Milton "Mickey" Rutner likely would have remained at shortstop had he been playing today. But after a single Class B season at short, the Athletics acquired him from the Tigers, moving him to third base for their Class B team in Wilmington, Delaware—likely because at 5'11", 190 pounds, he was a bit too big for shortstop at the time. (This was before baseball figured out it was okay to have power hitters at shortstop.)

Rutner grew into the role, hitting .300 or better three consecutive seasons and earning a call-up to Philadelphia in 1947. But he hit .250 in 48 at bats, and though he earned a spot on the 1948 opening day roster, Connie Mack soon shipped him back to AA Birmingham.

Rutner would have had a tough time breaking into that Philadelphia lineup anyway—Hank Majeski blocked him at third, and Eddie Joost was in the way at shortstop. Philadelphia had three straight winning seasons from 1947 to 1949, before losing 102 games in 1950 as the Phillies went to the World Series—a season that likely cost the Athletics the city.

Rutner put up solid batting averages into the early 1950s, hitting no worse than .274 in high-level minor leagues like the Texas League, Southern Association, and International League.

Rutner was, according to the Philadelphia A's Historical Society, the inspiration for Eliot Asinof's novel *Man on Spikes*. It is certain that Rutner worked as a greeter for the Round Rock Express well into his 80s.

### 4. Ike Samuels
*Bats Right, Throws Right*
*St. Louis Cardinals, 1895*

It would be hard to do less to impress in a brief major league trial than Ike Samuels did when signed off the streets of Chicago to play for the St. Louis Cardinals (then known as the St. Louis Brown Stockings). Samuels hit just .230/.278/.257 in a league that hit .296/.361/.400. He also made 20 errors in 21 games at third base, 4 in three games at shortstop.

The 1895 Brown Stockings were no attraction, finishing 39–92. But the park they played in, Robison Field, was roughly 100 years ahead of its time, with a huge amusement park beyond the left field stands. The team, however, would not achieve success on the field for another 31 years. Meanwhile, the St. Louis Browns of the American League, created in 1901, did not win a pennant until 1944.

Given the baseball being played in St. Louis, it is safe to say an amusement park was a very good idea.

## 5. Eddie Turchin

*Bats Right, Throws Right*
*Cleveland Indians, 1943*

Another player given a chance due to able-bodied shortages in World War II, Eddie Turchin got his cup of coffee with the Cleveland Indians.

It certainly didn't happen due to his bat. Though Turchin hit .295 with a .443 slugging percentage with the Class D Dominion Hawks of the famous Cape Breton Colliery League in 1937, he never slugged above .400 again, nor did he approach his .295 batting average. (It should be noted that the league, based in Canada, appears to have been a Jewish haven. According to *The Encyclopedia of Minor League Baseball*, the 1939 circuit leader in batting average and RBI was Abe Abramowitz, and the wins/ERA leader was Bernie Pearlman.)

Turchin played shortstop for the Eastern League champion Wilkes-Barre Barons in 1941 and returned to the infield in 1942, despite hitting .220 with a .246 slugging percentage. As the March 5, 1942, issue of *The Sporting News* described him, Turchin was "light-hitting, but superlative fielding." Sad that this did not become the common term, rather than "good-field, no-hit."

Turchin played four games at third and two at shortstop for the 1943 Indians. He committed just one error and hit .231/.375/.231. With the aforementioned Ken Keltner at third base (see Rosen, Al; shortened career due to) and the Jewish shortstop standard-bearer Lou Boudreau at shortstop, the Indians simply had no room for Turchin.

Turchin played for Buffalo in 1943 and Indianapolis in 1946, two high-level minor league teams. He fielded well for both (note that his high error total likely means he got to a lot more balls), and didn't hit much for either. In between, he helped the United States win a war and even hit a double for the Sampson Naval Training Center team in a 4–0 win over Cornell University in September 1944.

### 6. Henry Bostick

*Bats Right, Throws Right*
*Philadelphia Athletics, 1915*

Among Jewish players who changed their names, Henry Lipschitz to Henry Bostick has to be the most successful conversion. Henry Bostick could own a manor in Great Britain; Henry Lipschitz can get you that same ring wholesale.

There is little record of Bostick's playing career. According to SABR's minor league database, he played shortstop for Topeka of the Western League, hit .224 with a .295 slugging percentage, yet still earned a call-up to the Philadelphia A's early in the season. Maybe they wanted to give the British guy a chance.

He played May 18 and 19, 1915, but Philadelphia lost both games to slip into last place, where they finished. There were plenty of reasons why the four-time defending AL champs were slipping (Connie Mack selling off 75 percent of his "$100,000 infield," for instance), but Bostick was hardly a primary reason.

Bostick returned to Denver, where he had attended college. I like to think that until he passed away in 1968, he lived the life of landed gentry in the Rocky Mountains.

### 7. Steve Hertz
*Bats Right, Throws Right*
*Houston Colt .45s, 1964*

A pair of young infielders played sparingly for Houston in the franchise's third big league season. One of them simply couldn't get at bats behind Nellie Fox. The other was trapped behind Bob Aspromonte. Still, Houston stuck with the first guy but buried the second guy in the minors.

The first guy was Hall of Famer Joe Morgan. The second guy was Steve Hertz. In hindsight, Houston probably made the right call.

Hertz never got a start in his five games with Houston, appearing as part of a double switch twice, as a pinch hitter twice, and as a pinch runner once.

This pinch running, during a May 31, 1964, game against the Phillies, was Hertz's moment to shine. After Bob Aspromonte walked, Hertz pinch-ran and promptly took second base on a wild pitch. He advanced to third on a walk, though Aspromonte might well have done so, too. Hertz then scored on Al Spangler's infield single. He was promptly rewarded with a seat on the bench due to a double switch.

Hertz provided a mediocre batting average but above-average utility for the remainder of his minor league career with Houston and the New York Mets, playing second, short, and third. He played three full seasons in Florida and apparently liked it; he went on to coach at Miami Coral Park High School, then Miami-Dade College, where he coached players such as Placido Polanco and Omar Olivares.

He managed the Tel Aviv Lightning of the Israel Baseball League in 2007. If anything could prepare someone for managing in Israel, one would imagine it would have to be managing in Florida, between the temperate climate and the number of Jews. Judging by Tel Aviv's 26–14 record in the IBL's first season, his time in Florida served him well.

## 8. Phil Cooney
*Bats Left, Throws Right*
*New York Highlanders, 1905*
Don't let the Cooney fool you—Phil Cooney was actually Phil Cohen from New York. It is certainly an oddity to list Cooney among the third basemen. Though he played his one major league game at the position, going 0-for-3, he logged well over 1,700 career games in the minor leagues—roughly 1,000 at shortstop, 700 at second base—and according to the SABR record, not one at third base.

Cooney played for the Paterson (New Jersey) Intruders, an oddly prescient name, given the trend of that city over the subsequent 100 years toward crime, then was loaned to the soon-to-be-Yankees at the tail end of the 1905 season. At the start of the year, the Hal Chase–led squad was expected to contend for the American League pennant. But Chase slumped to .249, dissension ran deep within the ball club, and in a not-unusual result, the Highlanders fell in Cooney's one game, 7–2, to the St. Louis Browns.

Cooney returned to the Intruders in 1906 and batted .191, but he evidently contributed enough defensively to help Paterson to the Hudson River League title, narrowly edging out the Poughkeepsie Colts. (If the Hudson River League had existed 100 years later, when I went to school, there would have been nine minor league teams within 50 miles of the Bard College campus.)

Cooney went on to play for mostly A-level minor league teams. The New York boy headed to Portland, Oregon, Spokane, Washington, Sioux City, Iowa, Omaha, Nebraska, back east with the Jersey City Skeeters, then finished up out in Sioux City. Iowans got to see his best season in 1913, when he hit .300 with a .368 slugging percentage while learning a new position, second base.

Overall, Cooney was a useful middle infielder for well over a decade. And for a fleeting moment, Cohen, known as Cooney, became a hometown hero for the Highlanders, soon to be known as the Yankees, when the second baseman/shortstop became a third baseman for a day.

### 9. Joe Bennett
*Bats Right, Throws Right*
*Philadelphia Phillies, 1923*
Bennett had a Moonlight Graham career, getting an assist at third base for the Phillies on July 5, 1923, but never recording an at bat.

Had he been a pitcher, he might have stuck around—
Philadelphia lost that game, 16–12. The Phils went on to
allow 18 runs two days later, then had a three-game run of
21, 12, and 13 runs allowed. Even in the Baker Bowl, 1,008
runs is a lot to give up in a season.

| NAME | GAMES | AT BATS | OPS+ | WARP3 | Additional |
|------|-------|---------|------|-------|------------|
| 1. Al Rosen | 1044 | 3725 | 137 | 53.1 | 1953 AL MVP |
| 2. Cy Block | 17 | 53 | 113 | 0.7 | .354+ avg. 3 times in minors |
| 3. Mickey Rutner | 12 | 48 | 73 | 0.2 | |
| 4. Ike Samuels | 24 | 74 | 39 | −0.6 | 24 games, 24 errors |
| 5. Eddie Turchin | 11 | 13 | 83 | 0.1 | |
| 6. Henry Bostick | 2 | 7 | −62 | −0.2 | |
| 7. Steve Hertz | 5 | 4 | −100 | −0.1 | |
| 8. Phil Cooney | 1 | 3 | −100 | −0.1 | |
| 9. Joe Bennett | 1 | 0 | — | 0.0 | |

# 6

## *Shortstop*

**N**ot only is Lou Boudreau the greatest shortstop in Jewish baseball history, he is the greatest Jewish manager—and a good argument can be made that he is the greatest player, period. Not Sandy Koufax. Not Hank Greenberg.

There are two reasons, I believe, why this isn't often posited. For one thing, Koufax's and Greenberg's Jewish identities were much better known than Boudreau's—his mother was Jewish, but Boudreau was raised by his Christian father following a divorce. For another, Boudreau didn't have the eye-popping home run totals of Greenberg or strikeout totals of Koufax.

But take Baseball Prospectus's WARP3, which measures total value over a replacement player at a given position. For his career, Boudreau's value was at 110.1, due to a combination of strong offense and strong defense at shortstop, arguably the most important defensive position. Greenberg's total? 77.0. Koufax? 68.3. Shawn Green? 82.9. Al Rosen? 53.1.

Now, it is worth noting that Greenberg missed roughly four full seasons on the heels of putting up a 9.2 mark in 1940. Take away World War II, and Hank likely fights Boudreau to a draw in WARP3. Given the unreliable nature of fielding evaluations from that time, it is hard to give Boudreau the ultimate edge.

But he certainly should be in the conversation. And he seldom is.

The rest of the shortstops, however, are not in Greenberg territory, unless one is referring to Adam Greenberg, whose major league career consisted of one plate appearance where he was hit by a pitch.

### 1. Lou Boudreau
*Bats Right, Throws Right*
*Cleveland Indians, 1938–1950*
*Boston Red Sox, 1951–1952*
An interesting aspect of Lou Boudreau's career is that though the middle of his peak took place during World War II, and he played through the war in a weakened American League, he put up his best numbers before and after the war. Adjusted for league, of course, his 1943–1944–1945 numbers are among his strongest. His only two 100-RBI seasons came, however, in 1940 and 1948, and his three highest home run seasons were 1940, 1941, and 1948.

Boudreau's 1948 is sadly overlooked, since it is one of the most impressive seasons in baseball history. Judge it by OPS+, putting his offensive output in park and era context, and he is at 164, or 64 percent above average. That mark is sixth among shortstops since 1900, third since the end of the deadball era. Above it are only Robin Yount's MVP season in 1982 and Rico Petrocelli's 1969.

The more one looks at the numbers, the more impressive they are. In baseball, hitters fail much more often than they succeed, but Boudreau's 1948 might have been as close to a perfect foil for that truism as any single season. His season line was .355/.453/.534, and as a terrific defensive shortstop. He hit 18 home runs, drove in 106 runs, finished second in the league in batting average, second in on-base percentage, and fourth in slugging percentage. He walked 98 times, and—this is my favorite part—he struck out *nine times all season*. Twice as many home runs as strikeouts. To put this in perspective, Alex Rodriguez has, three times in his career, struck out four times in a single game.

Worth mentioning: as he was doing this on the field, he also managed Cleveland, leading them to their last World Series title. He hit .273/.333/.455 in the World Series.

He drove in a run as starting shortstop in the All-Star Game.

He had 16 sacrifice hits, fifth in the American League.

A corollary of Al Rosen's delay coming to the major leagues: the best Jewish third baseman didn't play much alongside the best Jewish shortstop. By 1950, Rosen's first full year at third base, Boudreau lost his job to Ray Boone, logging just 61 games at shortstop. By the next season, Boudreau was in Boston.

Boudreau, like Rosen, did not age well as a player. His all-world 1948 at age 30 was his last Hall of Fame season—he was average in 1949, a part-timer in 1950–1951, and finished in 1952. Still, he was elected to the Hall of Fame in 1970, due to both his playing days and his 1,162 wins as "Boy Manager." Amazingly, though he began managing at age 24, his last game as manager came at age 42, his last top 3 finish at age 31. He fit a whole Hall of Fame career into his first 31 years.

### 2. Jim Levey

*Bats Both, Throws Right*
*St. Louis Browns, 1930–1933*

One of the easiest mistakes for casual baseball fans to make is believing there is any correlation between errors and fielding prowess.

Errors are often assigned by official scorers on balls that are reached but not fielded cleanly. If Shortstop A reaches 100 more balls than Shortstop B but muffs 15 of them, Shortstop A is still immensely more valuable than Shortstop B is.

Well, Jim Levey had an 18-year career as a Shortstop A, making plenty of errors while adding tremendous defensive value to his teams. Levey displayed a fair amount of power as well in his three minor league seasons, putting up slugging percentages of .517, .425, and .440 in three stops before landing with the St. Louis Browns late in the 1930 season.

Levey was quite the athlete: despite being cautioned by Willis E. Johnson in the November 20, 1930, edition of *The Sporting News* not to "forever mar his baseball career" by taking the injury risk, he went on to play several off-seasons with the Pittsburgh Steelers of the NFL.

In 1931, though he hit .209/.264/.285 (a ridiculously poor total in any era, let alone in the high-scoring early 1930s), Levey took hold of the shortstop job in St. Louis, despite an AL-high 58 errors. His "flashy fielding" earned him high marks in *The Sporting News*' January 1932 Browns season preview. Again, errors are a rotten way to evaluate fielders.

His hitting even took a temporary turn forward, and he appeared ready to become one of the league's top shortstops in 1932. His hot start, which the May 12, 1932, *Sporting News* credited to his switch-hitting, had him at .346, third in the American League. But the average faded; he ended the season at .280, which placed him seventh on his own team. Still, his average and his defense led to his being listed on five MVP ballots, good for a 19th-place finish—tied with Hall of Famer Ted Lyons and ahead of Hall of Famer Joe Sewell.

It appears the league figured out how to pitch to both the left- and right-handed Levey. In 1933 Levey put up a .195/.237/.240 line. The total OPS+ was 24—the lowest single-season mark of any starting shortstop from 1901 to 2008. With offensive expectations for shortstops now much higher, that 24 OPS+ is probably as unbreakable a baseball record as Cy Young's 511 career victories.

Levey was traded to the Pacific Coast League's Hollywood Stars, along with two other players, for Alan Strange, his replacement at shortstop. He played for Hollywood for two seasons (alongside a number of major leaguers, such as Vince DiMaggio and Hall of Famer Bobby Doerr), then headed to the Texas League. Levey continued to put up reasonable offense and eye-popping error totals until 1945, missing a season in 1943 to serve the U.S. war cause.

He certainly didn't keep his spot in professional baseball because of his hitting, overall. And as observers doubtlessly could see at the time, his fielding should not be judged by his errors.

### 3. Murray Franklin

*Bats Right, Throws Right*
*Detroit Tigers, 1941–1942*

Murray Franklin might have had a fine major league career, but two interruptions, one of his own making, prevented it.

Franklin displayed a plus bat after joining the Detroit Tigers' organization in 1937. He had a decent D-level debut for Beckley of the Mountain State League, then dominated in his second season on the circuit, hitting .439 with 26 home runs in 385 at bats, good for a .790 slugging percentage. Two seasons in Beaumont followed, where Hank Greenberg had been Texas League MVP earlier in the decade. Franklin posted .288 and .290 batting averages, with slugging percentages of .393 and .396—very good for a shortstop at that time.

By 1941, after a terrific season (.291 average, .428 slugging percentage) for Little Rock of the Southern Association, he debuted for the Tigers. In 13 at bats he hit .300 and followed with a respectable .260/.301/.344 line for the 1942 Tigers while splitting the shortstop job with Billy Hitchcock, who hit just .211.

But the war called Franklin away. To compound matters, he was lured by the higher salaries to the Mexican League in 1946. Organized baseball banned all players who jumped to the Mexican League, and Franklin didn't return to American baseball until 1949, when he joined the Hollywood Stars of the Pacific Coast League.

Franklin was now 35 and no longer covered enough ground to play short. But he played another five seasons in the PCL for three teams, even blasting 13 home runs in 311 at bats for Hollywood in 1951. Had postwar baseball salaries been higher, and had Neville Chamberlain's appeasement policies worked, Franklin likely would have had similar seasons in the big leagues.

### 4. Eddie Zosky

*Bats Right, Throws Right*
*Toronto Blue Jays, 1991–1992*
*Florida Marlins, 1995*
*Milwaukee Brewers, 1999*
*Houston Astros, 2000*

Nearly all of us have been set up on blind dates by well-meaning relatives. (If this hasn't happened to you, approximate the experience by stabbing yourself in the thigh with a garden hoe.) The prospective date is talked up in a way that makes him or her sound absolutely perfect, yet the date itself goes horribly, horribly wrong.

This is essentially Eddie Zosky's career. His scouting report, I assume, went something like this:

"Have I got a shortstop for you! His name is Eddie Zosky, he's from California. Both *The Sporting News* and *Baseball America* named him an All-American at Fresno State! A nice Jewish shortstop for you, with a plus arm and fantastic range!

"He's still on the market—the Mets drafted him, but it didn't work out. If I were you, I'd sign him for a bonus of $182,000 and bring him home—your family will love him."

And of course, the awkward conversation afterward is even worse than the date itself.

"So? How'd it go? Is he at the top of your lineup? . . . Really? Only .160 over five major league seasons? I'm surprised . . . well, you only gave him 50 at bats. He was probably great in the minors . . . just .256? With a .292 on-base? That doesn't sound like him at all. He was *Baseball America*'s 22nd-ranked prospect in 1991! . . . yes, I know he dropped to 82nd in 1992, and then off the list, but he did hurt his elbow . . . wow, I don't think changing uniform numbers five times shows a lack of commitment, but okay . . . no, I'm not upset. If you don't want a shortstop because he can't hit, that's fine.

I just see other girls your age with a full lineup, adding to their bench, and I wanted to help. Suit yourself!"

### 5. Jonah Goldman
*Bats Right, Throws Right*
*Cleveland Indians, 1928, 1930–1931*

All indications are that Jonah Goldman was simply not able to hit major league pitching consistently. His career line was .224/.293/.283, and he was given 306 at bats in 1930 alone to prove otherwise—his line for the season was .242/.312/.310, which is substandard in any season, but particularly 1930, the Year of the Hitter. The league's line? .288/.351/.421.

But even by October 1931, Goldman's devotees hadn't given up, though Cleveland had.

"With the exception of Jonah Goldman, the Indians haven't had a shortstop candidate who showed any aptitude for the job," Ed Bang wrote in the October 22, 1931, edition of *The Sporting News*. "Goldman was really a great fielder. His failure to make the grade as a batter upset him so that he did not turn in his customary sparkling defensive performance early last season, and the powers decided they would definitely give up hope of Goldman proving the answer to their greatest need. Jonah has his admirers, however, and they will tell you that the little Jewish lad, if assured the position were his, would become not only a positive sensation as a fielder, but would step to the plate with sufficient confidence to bring him a respectable batting average."

There you have it, folks. Anyone who tries to castigate

today's media for relying on anonymous sources doesn't know what he or she is talking about. Back in 1931, it was deemed appropriate to quote Jonah Goldman's mother.

## 6. Eddie Feinberg
*Bats Both, Throws Right*
*Philadelphia Phillies, 1938–1939*

While the sabermetric movement has taken huge leaps forward in the past 25 years, it is still nearly impossible to prove that a player's performance is affected by God. Think of it like clutch hitting: the battle over existence makes it impossible to quantify.

That said, if such a measurement ever becomes possible, expect sabermetricians to look hard at Eddie Feinberg. After dropping out of high school to play for Centreville in the Eastern Shore League, Feinberg finished with a .334 average, 15 home runs, and 80 RBI in 1937, and earned a look by the Philadelphia Phillies. At age 20, his future in baseball seemed bright.

According to *The Big Book of Jewish Baseball*, Feinberg chose to play on Yom Kippur late in the 1938 season, while Jewish teammates Phil Weintraub and Morrie Arnovich elected to sit out. Feinberg played, went 0-for-8, and "regretted the decision for the rest of his life."

The only problem with this story is that it didn't happen. Yom Kippur in 1938 began at sundown on October 4, after the season ended. The story can't even have been on Rosh Hashanah, 1938—the Phillies were off that day. And while they played a doubleheader on Rosh Hashanah eve, 1938, in the prelights days of baseball, sundown, which is when the holiday starts, was also when the games had to end.

The Phils did play a doubleheader on Yom Kippur, 1939—but Weintraub was no longer with Philadelphia, and neither was Feinberg; he'd been dealt to the Chicago White Sox, who buried him in the minor leagues.

Feinberg finished his professional career with stints in St. Paul, Scranton, and Greenville, South Carolina, among other teams. He never approached his Centreville numbers. But it does not appear that God, in this case, was to blame.

### 7. Lou Brower
*Bats Right, Throws Right*
*Detroit Tigers, 1931*
While Julio Franco earned acclaim from "forever young" stories as a 49-year-old pinch hitter in 2007 for the Mets, his ability to play the field was severely compromised. But Lou Brower managed to play second base as a 47-year-old.

Granted, it was in the Sooner State League. But he did well enough that, in conjunction with a .259 batting average and .329 slugging percentage, he was able to play/manage the Lawton Giants to a regular-season title.

Brower's career began 22 years earlier, with the London Indians of the Michigan-Ontario League. His game didn't change much over the two decades. He hit over .300 four times, along with seasons of .288, .291, and .296. He reached double figures in triples eight times, the final time at age 37 for Oklahoma City of the Texas League. He even hit a triple in his age-47 season.

Brower managed into his 50s in the Sooner State League, reaching the playoffs six times.

But during his six weeks in the major leagues, the hits didn't fall. Brower took over at shortstop for the Detroit Tigers in June 1931, got 62 at bats, but batted just .161. It doesn't appear he was overmatched—eight walks, just five strikeouts—but six weeks was all he got. The younger and more talented Billy Rogell took over, hit .303, and held on to the position until 1938.

Still, it is hard to say that Brower was cheated. And he certainly made up for his brief tenure in the majors with his minor league volume.

## 8. Al Richter
*Bats Right, Throws Right*
*Boston Red Sox, 1951, 1953*
Al Richter never hit much in the minor leagues. That the Boston Red Sox continued to promote him speaks awfully well of his defensive prowess.

He hit .256 for the D-level Oneonta Red Sox—and promptly got promoted to Class C Lynn. He hit .238 for Lynn—and got ushered up to Scranton, where he hit .225. And he continued up the ladder.

In 1951, Richter finally hit, to the tune of .321 for Louisville of the Eastern League.

So he finally got to Boston in September 1951, and the

Red Sox certainly didn't need a shortstop—Johnny Pesky hit .313 with a .417 on-base percentage that season.

Richter continued his career-long ability to not hit, logging a .091 average. He did play three games at short, turning 5 double plays, made 10 putouts, and added 8 assists. While it is an impossibly small sample, he logged all three categories at a much higher rate than the starter Pesky.

Richter returned to the minors for four more seasons, hitting between .248 and .277, with anemic slugging percentages between .304 and .327. But he still logged 564 games over four seasons. Richter's glove carried him to the majors—and provided him with a 10-year minor league career.

### 9. Jesse Baker
*Bats Right, Throws Right*
*Washington Senators, 1919*

Jesse Baker played in the late-teens South. After his one game for the 1919 Washington Senators, he headed to the Richmond Colts of the Virginian League, then to the Danville Tobbaconists in Virginia of the Piedmont League.

This was the South, less than a decade after a lynch mob had kidnapped and murdered the Jewish businessman Leo Frank over a murder he pretty clearly didn't commit. Half of Georgia's Jews left the state afterward. The other half, as far as I can tell, were the subject of the film *Driving Miss Daisy*.

You'd have changed your name to Jesse Baker, too.

One important footnote to Jesse Baker's career: in his one plate appearance for the Senators, on September 14, 1919, Baker hit a sacrifice fly, driving in a run. Yet he did not earn the nickname "the Human Sacrifice Fly," for reasons that are unclear.

## 10. Reuben Ewing
*Bats Right, Throws Right*
*St. Louis Cardinals, 1921*
Would you believe only three major leaguers ever are from Odessa, Ukraine? And all three were Jewish?

Ewing, who decided to stick with the Jewish first name but change to Ewing from Cohen, was one of the three, and the only position player. Pitcher Bill Cristall preceded him by 20 years—clearly, he did not look marvelous in his 48 innings of 4.84 ERA pitching. And Izzy Goldstein came along in 1932, walked 41, struck out just 14, and returned to the minors.

But both pitchers enjoyed substantial minor league careers. There is no playing record of Ewing, outside of his time at Lebanon Valley College and three games with St. Louis. He struck out in his only at bat.

| NAME | GAMES | AT BATS | OPS+ | WARP3 | Additional |
|------|-------|---------|------|-------|------------|
| 1. Lou Boudreau | 1646 | 6029 | 120 | 110.1 | 8-time All-Star, 1948 MVP |
| 2. Jim Levey | 440 | 1632 | 48 | −4.6 | |
| 3. Murray Franklin | 61 | 164 | 78 | 0.5 | War prevented real career |

| NAME | GAMES | AT BATS | OPS+ | WARP3 | Additional |
|------|-------|---------|------|-------|------------|
| 4. Eddie Zosky | 44 | 50 | 14 | −0.2 | |
| 5. Jonah Goldman | 148 | 349 | 45 | 0.9 | |
| 6. Eddie Feinberg | 16 | 38 | 20 | −0.1 | |
| 7. Lou Brower | 21 | 62 | 20 | −0.5 | |
| 8. Al Richter | 6 | 11 | 2 | 0.1 | |
| 9. Jesse Baker | 1 | 0 | — | 0.0 | |
| 10. Reuben Ewing | 3 | 1 | −100 | 0.0 | |

## 7

## *Left Field*

There appears to be a changing of the guard coming in left field. For the better part of 50 years, Sid Gordon has been the undisputed champion among Jewish left fielders. Gordon had five Hall of Fame–caliber seasons, along with another few huge years as a part-time player. Gordon's WARP3, according to Baseball Prospectus, was 63.6, putting him within hailing distance of Hank Greenberg.

Like Greenberg, he missed time for the war, although just two seasons, to Greenberg's four. But they were his age-26 and age-27 seasons, likely to have been among his finest. He's not the best Jewish player ever, but he isn't that far off.

Ryan Braun, two seasons into his major league career with the Milwaukee Brewers, though, is putting up numbers that dwarf Gordon's seasons, at least superficially.

*Sid Gordon*

Gordon's best two slugging percentages were .537 and .557—
in Braun's rookie year, his slugging was .634, and in 2008,
he stood at .553.

Still, once adjusting for era, it isn't clear that Braun's 2007
was better than Gordon's best season. Braun's 2007 OPS+
was 153, while Gordon's best mark, in 1950, was 156.

The remarkable aspect of Braun's season was that it came
in his very first exposure to the major leagues. He had just
767 minor league at bats and was just 23 years old when he
put up that season.

Gordon has to be rated ahead of Braun as of now. But if
Braun merely continues at this rate, he'll blow Gordon away
before he's 30. And if he improves any (considering that his
defense in left field is average, rather than comically bad, as
it was at third base), Braun will soon be in the Greenberg/
Koufax discussion.

### 1. Sid Gordon

*Bats Right, Throws Right*
*New York Giants, 1941–1949*
*Boston Braves, 1950–1952*
*Milwaukee Braves, 1953*
*Pittsburgh Pirates, 1954–1955*
*New York Giants, 1955*

My favorite aspect of Sid Gordon's career is that he played
the majority of his career with the New York Giants, was
never a Brooklyn Dodger, yet was honored at Ebbets Field.
How is this possible? He wasn't a Sal Maglie, who came to

the Dodgers late in his career and won the fans over. He wasn't a member of the team!

A reasonable guess as to why Gordon was so favorably received, even though he played for the orange and black, can be made based on this fact, reported by Dan Daniel in the December 29, 1954, issue of *The Sporting News:* "If the data available in the Brooklyn business office, compiled from the advance sales lists, is reliable, more than 50 percent of the club's patronage is made up of Jewish fans."

This is an astounding fact, if it is even close to true. It also redoubles the tragedy that struck when Walter O'Malley moved the team from Brooklyn, taking the great Sandy Koufax from his Jewish fan base in New York.

But the double-edged sword that Gordon faced throughout his career, due to his identification as Jewish, may be apparent in a pair of lists by writers in *The Sporting News.* One list, from January 6, 1954, has Gordon on the "Most Conceited" team, along with fellow Jews Cal Abrams and Saul Rogovin. Really? Three out of 16? A good 19 percent? Seems high, no? Perhaps people thought the three demurred from eating ham because it would go right to their hips.

Gordon was also one of 3 Jewish players out of 16 voted by the writers as having "Best Business Sense" in a poll published on March 30, 1955, along with Al Rosen and Abrams—a bit stereotypical for my taste.

At least for Gordon, they also named him most relaxed, happiest, most generous, most helpful to rookies, and, of course, sees most movies.

## 2. Ryan Braun

*Bats Right, Throws Right*
*Milwaukee Brewers, 2007–*

Braun has had a meteoric rise but is a very down-to-earth player. It would have been easy to lose one's head as one of the finest offensive players in baseball, less than three years removed from being drafted, but Braun has a journeyman attitude.

What is astounding, now that Braun has found a position, is how difficult it is to find anything he doesn't do well, with the obvious exception of drawing walks. But Braun appears to hit for a high enough average, and with enough power, that his on-base percentage isn't likely to suffer—and as teams around the league decide they'd rather not pitch to him, that number will likely be going up, too.

Despite just 71 walks in his first 1,062 at bats, Braun has a .350 on-base percentage, a consequence of his .301 batting average. He hits a fine .283/.327/.546 against righties, but against lefties, he is peak Ted Williams, .351/.412/.702. Milwaukee is a hitter's park, and his home line is .314/.371/.641, but he puts up a .290/.330/.538 line away, too.

Hank Greenberg's age-23 season was similar to Braun's rookie season, though in Hank's case it was his second full year in the big leagues. He put up a line of .339/.404/.600, with 26 home runs in 593 at bats. His OPS+ was 156, just above Braun's 2007 stat of 153.

Hank Greenberg was one of the finest hitters of all time. If Braun can stay at his current levels, he may just surpass Greenberg.

## 3. Morrie Arnovich

*Bats Right, Throws Right*
*Philadelphia Phillies, 1936–1940*
*Cincinnati Reds, 1940*
*New York Giants, 1941, 1946*

It's the age-old dilemma: baseball player or rabbi? Rabbi or baseball player? Morrie Arnovich, who was encouraged to become a rabbi by his parents, chose ballplayer instead. And while Arnovich was not the player either Gordon or Braun was, he certainly provided value to his teams during a career that was cut nearly in half by World War II. He managed a career line of .287/.350/.383, while providing plus defense, and had a season in 1939 that landed him on the All-Star team.

Arnovich was actually one of three Jews in that 1939 All-Star Game; the other two were Hank Greenberg and Harry Danning. Arnovich was among the league leaders in hitting all season, finishing fifth, behind Hall of Famers Johnny Mize, Paul Waner, and Ducky Medwick, as well as Frank McCormick, who would be named NL MVP the following season.

His season also led the Phillies, who, in fairness, were en route to finishing 45–106 and needed any distraction, to hold "Morrie Arnovich Day" on July 16, 1939. Arnovich was provided "a complete and up-to-date fishing outfit," according to the July 20, 1939, issue of *The Sporting News*.

And, the paper reported, one Charles Arnovich, father of Morrie, was in the stands, cheerfully supporting his son.

## 4. Guy Zinn

*Bats Left, Throws Right*
*New York Yankees, 1911–1912*
*Boston Braves, 1913*
*Baltimore Terrapins, 1914–1915*

Baltimore Terrapins? That's right, it was part of the Federal League, one of the periodic attempts to create a third major league to compete with the National and American circuits.

Zinn had a very solid career in the three years he spent in the major leagues, the two years spent in the Federal League, and the seasons that followed in the minors, where many Federal League players went when the league folded following the 1915 season. Each season from 1912 to 1915, Zinn's OPS+ improved, from 106, to 107, 111, and 114.

Four above-average seasons of production is impressive, but Zinn couldn't find his way back to the big leagues, with the Federal League taint no doubt playing a part.

Instead, he made his way to the Class B New York State League, where he hit .260. He wandered from Bridgeport, Connecticut, to Newark, New Jersey, and Jersey City, finally finding his hitting stroke again with the Hamilton Tigers of the Michigan-Ontario League, where he posted a pair of .300 seasons in 1919–1920. He even tried pitching when his bat gave out, and there is record of Zinn both pitching and hitting in the Class D Piedmont League in 1929, when he was 42 years old. It didn't go well; his ERA was 6.10, though he did hit .273 in 36 at bats.

Zinn certainly charted a unique course for himself—not surprising, for a Jewish man in West Virginia.

## 5. Don Taussig

*Bats Right, Throws Right*
*San Francisco Giants, 1958*
*St. Louis Cardinals, 1961*
*Houston Colt .45s, 1962*

Don Taussig slaved for eight years in the minor leagues so he could play for his hometown New York Giants, only to get his chance in 1958, when the Giants were clear across the country.

Taussig's development was interrupted by service in the Korean War, and you can see the effect. He hit .263 with a .396 slugging percentage for Class A Jacksonville in 1952 as a 20-year-old, but after returning from the war, he hit just .210 in his first time with AA Dallas and was sent down to Sioux City for more seasoning.

By 1957 he'd made good in Dallas, hitting 22 home runs, batting .281, and slugging .464. To put his performance in perspective, Willie McCovey had nearly identical rate stats, batting .281 and slugging .463. Of course, this was Taussig's third season in Dallas, McCovey's first, and McCovey was four years younger.

Still, one didn't have to hit like Willie McCovey to be a serviceable major leaguer, but Taussig had trouble breaking into San Francisco's outfield of Willie Mays, Leon Wagner, Felipe Alou, McCovey, Willie Kirkland ... no easy feat.

He was sent to the Portland Beavers of the Pacific Coast League, a high-level minor league, and thrived, hitting .286/.350/.500 with 23 home runs and 101 RBI.

The Cardinals acquired him, and he faced a similar logjam in the outfield, with Stan Musial, Curt Flood, and Joe Cunningham. He held his own with the Cardinals, posting a season line of .287/.338/.447, which got him drafted by Houston in the expansion draft. But Houston gave him just 25 at bats, perhaps because at age 30 he was no longer a prospect.

The timing was never quite right for Don Taussig, an outfielder with power.

## 6. Alta Cohen
*Bats Left, Throws Left*
*Brooklyn Dodgers, 1931–1932*
*Philadelphia Phillies, 1934*

Had *The Jazz Singer* been written a decade later, it could have been made about a baseball player, rather than a jazz singer. You'd probably have had to change the name of the movie, of course. But that ballplayer could have been Alta Cohen.

Cohen's father, a Newark rabbi, renamed him Alta, meaning "old," during the 1918 flu epidemic to protect him, according to Martin Abramowitz, the outstanding Jewish baseball scholar.

Cohen actually did the same thing during his baseball career, reinventing himself impressively. At the start of his career, he was an outfielder. He posted a .335 batting average and .460 slugging percentage with the Macon Peaches of the Class A South Atlantic League, then followed with a .316 batting average and .448 slugging for the Hartford Senators of the Eastern League, earning a call-up by the Brooklyn Dodgers.

But by 1932, Cohen had trouble breaking into a very good Dodger outfield, and he didn't help matters with a .156 batting average. He showed he had nothing to prove when he returned to Hartford, hitting .412 in 226 at bats, though he was only at .249 after being promoted to AAA Jersey City.

After catching on for a year with the Class B Durham Bulls, Cohen got another big league chance by hitting .333 with a .441 slugging for the AA Toledo Mud Hens. He moved up to the Phillies but unfortunately hit .188 in 32 at bats, and the major league portion of his career was complete.

That's when Alta Cohen decided to become a pitcher. In 1935 for Toledo, he hit .279 in 452 at bats, but he also appeared in 11 games as a pitcher, including 6 starts, posting a 4–3, 4.58 ERA mark. For comparison, Roxie Lawson, who had a 10-year big league career, posted a 14–8, 3.92 ERA season for Toledo.

Cohen was a full-time pitcher in 1936, posting a 14–12, 5.21 ERA season. He improved on that in 1937, with a 15–7, 4.18 ERA year, and earned this praise in the June 17, 1937, issue of *The Sporting News:* "A bright spot for [manager Fred] Haney is the way his veteran performers are showing up.

Alta Cohen, versatile southpaw hurler . . . has pitched some magnificent games."

Cohen's transition was complete. And as for his father's wish in naming him Alta? Cohen died in Maplewood, New Jersey, at the ripe alta age of 94.

## 7. Brian Horwitz

*Bats Right, Throws Right*
*San Francisco Giants, 2008–*

Very little had been expected of Brian Horwitz, who has already exceeded those expectations since signing with the San Francisco Giants as an undrafted free agent in 2004.

Undrafted free agents don't usually win batting titles, but Horwitz hit .347 in his first season to win the Northwest League crown. He hit .349 in 2005 for Augusta of the South Atlantic League. By 2007 he put up a .320/.379/.418 line between AA and AAA. But he didn't have the power to earn a call-up to the majors.

So he went out in 2008 and hit for power. After a career high of 4 home runs, Horwitz hit 5 in his first 136 minor league at bats. An injury to Dan Ortmeier cleared the way for Horwitz.

He earned a start against the Mets on June 2, 2008, and New York announcer Gary Cohen pointed out that Horwitz was a line-drive hitter with little power. Horwitz hit his first major league home run on the very next pitch.

Before he was sent down on June 30, Horwitz posted a .222/.310/.389 line with a pair of home runs. It was a respectable effort for a first-time look at big league pitching, and Horwitz should get another opportunity at least.

## 8. Al Silvera
*Bats Right, Throws Right*
*Cincinnati Red Legs, 1955–1956*

For those Jewish parents who wish to use bedtime stories for instruction, allow me to present a ready-to-use "stay in school" cautionary tale: Al Silvera.

Once upon a time, there was a big right-handed slugger named Al Silvera. He was a high school star at Fairfax High in Los Angeles and made his parents very happy by not only going to college, but choosing the University of Southern California, which was very close and allowed him to visit his parents every chance he got.

But after his freshman year, the big bad Cincinnati Red Legs came along and offered Al $50,000 and a car to leave school without his degree. Al decided to take the money, not realizing that time with his family is priceless. The car came in handy, since he was running over his mother's shattered dreams.

Due to the size of his bonus, according to major league rules at that time, Al had to spend the whole year in Cincinnati, which is bad enough, but he got only 13 at bats, which is even worse. He returned to the minors in 1956 but hit only .197 in Port Arthur and Abilene, though he did get hits every time he called home. But because he never graduated college, Al never figured that part out.

By 1958 Al hit just .218 for the Albany Senators of the Eastern League and was released. He came back to California with his money and tried to buy back the time he'd lost with his family. But that time was all gone. Then he tried to buy some precious memories from college. But those, too, were beyond his reach.

If only Al had stayed in school, and gotten his degree, not only would he have lived the life of a famous professional baseball player . . . he'd have made his mother happy.

| NAME | GAMES | AT BATS | OPS+ | WARP3 | Additional |
|---|---|---|---|---|---|
| 1. Sid Gordon | 1475 | 4992 | 129 | 63.6 | 5 seasons over 140 OPS+ |
| 2. Ryan Braun | 264 | 1062 | 138 | 14.6 | Next stop: Hank Greenberg |
| 3. Morrie Arnovich | 590 | 2013 | 99 | 19.5 | .324 average in 1939 |
| 4. Guy Zinn | 314 | 1103 | 108 | 1.3 | |
| 5. Don Taussig | 153 | 263 | 84 | 1.9 | |
| 6. Alta Cohen | 29 | 67 | 41 | −0.1 | A pitcher, too! |
| 7. Brian Horwitz | 21 | 36 | 83 | 0.5 | |
| 8. Al Silvera | 14 | 7 | −25 | −0.1 | |

**8**

# Center Field

Center field is the hardest to rank Jewish players. Four men have good claims on the top spot, each from a different era, and each with different strengths.

Lipman Pike was the very first Jewish player in professional baseball and performed admirably in the National Association, the National League, and the American Association. He put up tremendous offensive numbers and certainly would be a fine choice at the position.

Goody Rosen had arguably the best single season of any Jewish center fielder, in 1945, and combined stellar defense and plate discipline in a 15-year major and minor league career.

Gabe Kapler played a pivotal sub role for the 2004 world champion Boston Red Sox, but he appeared headed to an even bigger major league career when he had three double-digit

*Elliott Maddox*

home run seasons for the Texas Rangers by age 25. After a year as a minor league manager, Kapler came out of retirement in 2008 and added to his already impressive career line.

But my choice as the finest of all Jewish center fielders is Elliott Maddox. The midcareer Jewish convert had terrific defense and plate discipline, like Rosen. He played for a World Series team, the 1976 Yankees. And though Pike's career line is far better than Maddox's, Pike played in far shorter seasons, giving Maddox about 25 percent more at bats, even though Pike played 16 seasons to Maddox's 11.

Maddox also provided versatility, with three games or more logged at first base, second base, and shortstop and 75 or more in left field, third base, right field, and, of course, center field.

Maddox also went to Union High School, where my parents went. Tie goes to the New Jersey product.

### 1. Elliott Maddox
*Bats Right, Throws Right*
*Detroit Tigers, 1970*
*Washington Senators, 1971*
*Texas Rangers, 1972–1973*
*New York Yankees, 1974–1976*
*Baltimore Orioles, 1977*
*New York Mets, 1978–1980*
It is important to note that Elliott Maddox's career line was more negatively affected by both his pitcher-friendly era and parks than any other Jewish center fielder's. His

career line was .261/.358/.334—neutralize it, and it climbs to .286/.388/.361, an OPS increase of 57 points.

A couple of interesting notes on Maddox: he was a decent base stealer for much of his career, succeeding 54 of 86 times through 1977. That is a success rate of 63 percent, a bit below ideal but not terrible. But during his three seasons with the Mets, he managed just 6 of 22 times to make it safely, an inexcusably bad 27 percent success rate. It is hard to understand such a decline, or why manager Joe Torre didn't give him a stop sign, but it lowered his career rate to under 53 percent.

Another fun fact: Maddox converted to Judaism for the 1974 season, on the heels of a .238/.356/.262 season. His line jumped to .303/.395/.386 in 1974 and continued through 55 games of .307/.382/.394 in 1975, before Maddox injured his knee at Shea Stadium.

This begs the question: does converting to Judaism midcareer improve one's line by 69 points of average, 26 points of on-base, and 132 points of slugging? Here is a look at some other players and their improvement had they converted midcareer to Judaism:

**VALUE-ADDED JUDAISM**
Babe Ruth, 1927: .425/.512/.904
Ted Williams, 1941: .475/.579/.867
Mario Mendoza, 1979: .267/.242/.381

Ruth and Williams become video-game good, and even Mario Mendoza becomes a pretty decent option at shortstop. With the stricter drug testing in the wake of the steroids scandals, players simply need to look to our synagogues as the new way to juice.

## 2. Lipman Pike

*Bats Left, Throws Left*
*Troy Haymakers, 1871*
*Baltimore Canaries, 1872–1873*
*Hartford Dark Blues, 1874*
*St. Louis Brown Stockings, 1875–1876*
*Cincinnati Reds, 1877–1878*
*Providence Grays, 1878*
*Worcester Ruby Legs, 1881*
*New York Metropolitans, 1887*

If you base evaluation of Pike against the other center fielders on reputation of the time, Pike clearly would have to be the number one choice. According to the SABR biography of Pike by Robert H. Schafer, Pike was named one of the three best outfielders of 1870–1880 by *Sporting Life* in 1911, 18 years after his death, and 25 years after that, even received a Hall of Fame vote on the very first Cooperstown ballots of 1936.

But while Pike clearly excelled in the time he played, it simply isn't clear how that success translates into ability. Take his total games played: 70 was his season high, and he had just five years with more than 50.

Then there are the questions about his honesty. Pike was accused by his team in 1881 of throwing games and suspended by organized baseball for a time. Earlier in his career, he was accused of disloyalty to his Philadelphia club, though it was assigned to his being a foreigner (from New York). Still, it is hard not to see these two issues as related.

Even things like Pike's reputation as a power hitter come with all kinds of caveats. He hit 4 home runs for Cincinnati in 1877, but the Reds' Lakefront Park was 180 feet down the left field line, 196 to right field—less than my Little League park's dimensions.

Take Pike's most famous game, in 1866 for the Philadelphia Athletics, prior to the formation of professional leagues. He hit 6 home runs! The final score: 67–25.

All in all, there is ample evidence to credit Lipman Pike with a very good career. Comparing between eras is difficult, to be sure. Ultimately, the preponderance of the available evidence gives the edge, in my mind, to Maddox.

### 3. Goody Rosen
*Bats Left, Throws Left*
*Brooklyn Dodgers, 1937–1939, 1944–1946*
*New York Giants, 1946*

Another example of Can-Jew spirit, it is fairly shocking that Goody Rosen didn't get more of an opportunity to play regularly in the major leagues.

Rosen started his career in 1932 with the Stroudsburg Poconos of the Interstate League (Class D) and quickly earned a promotion to the AA Eastern League. He then languished with Louisville for five long years, hitting between .293 and .314, showing tremendous plate discipline, and slugging between .377 and .444, while fielding his position extremely well. Yet it wasn't until the tail end of 1937 that Rosen got a chance in the major leagues.

Unlike others profiled, Rosen took immediate advantage of his opportunity. He hit .312/.361/.403 in 1937 and should have cemented his role with Brooklyn with his 1938 season. In his first full season in the majors, Rosen hit .281/.368/.389, with 65 walks against just 43 strikeouts. His offensive numbers were good for an OPS+ of 106, better than 15 of the 23 other National League starting outfielders.

Given that he could play all three outfield positions, and excelled at all of them, it is hard to believe that in 1939, the Dodgers benched Rosen in favor of Ernie Koy (OPS+ 105), Art Parks (OPS+ 86), and Gene Moore (OPS+ 72). Rosen's production came down a bit, but as a young player coming off a solid season, how was he not given more of a chance to straighten out? Instead, he spent much of the year at AAA Montreal, where, surprise, surprise, he hit .302 with a .426 slugging percentage.

The Dodgers rewarded him by selling him to Pittsburgh, and the Pirates buried him in the minors for four years. Rosen posted .282, .290, .263, and .276 averages during those years, with decent pop, and plus defense in AAA Syracuse. Finally, with the war taking a toll on players, Rosen got another chance to play with Brooklyn. He had a middling 1944 but took off in 1945.

Rosen's line was .325/.379/.460. He finished 3rd in batting average, 6th in slugging percentage, and 10th in on-base percentage. A rarity for a player who draws a fair amount of walks, Rosen finished second in the league in hits. He made the All-Star team and finished 10th in the league in MVP voting for a third-place team. According to the June 14, 1945, edition of *The Sporting News*, he even had two walk-off hits to defeat the archrival Giants—a two-run homer on June 5 and a game-winning single on April 28.

The Dodgers, however, had a surplus of outfielders, so Rosen was dealt to the rival Giants. He put up terrific numbers, hitting .281/.377/.390, which in the offense-starved 1946 season was good for a 117 OPS+. He was a bright spot for the disappointing Giants, who, perhaps aware that they weren't going to draw fans with wins, put together a team with five Jewish players: Rosen, Morrie Arnovich, Harry Feldman, Mike Schemer, and Sid Gordon. Rosen also deployed his clutch abilities against Brooklyn: on July 5, he hit a game-winning single to beat his former team.

Rosen ended his career in 1947 with a victory lap in Toronto, his hometown, putting up a .274 average and .369 slugging percentage with the AAA Maple Leafs. He was 35 and had lost his best seasons to the minors. His career OPS+ was 111, higher than current players such as Jeff Francoeur, Jose Cruz Jr., Mike Cameron, Xavier Nady, Garret Anderson, and Torii Hunter. And he was the defensive equivalent of any of them.

### 4. Gabe Kapler
*Bats Right, Throws Right*
*Detroit Tigers, 1998–1999*
*Texas Rangers, 2000–2002*

*Colorado Rockies, 2002–2003*
*Boston Red Sox, 2003–2006*
*Milwaukee Brewers, 2008–*

Where are you, Jewish mothers? Shawn Green joked with me about receiving marriage proposals from Jewish mothers and daughters everywhere he went. So I figured Kapler, whose shirtless physique landed him on the cover of many body-building magazines before he even reached the majors, had a succession of Jewish moms throwing stones at his window.

"No," Kapler said, standing at his locker following an April 2008 win over the Mets at Shea Stadium. "I never had anything like that."

I told him not to take it personally.

Like Fred Sington, Kapler has been able to translate his strength into monumental minor league numbers, but only sporadic power in the major leagues. His finest minor league season came with AA Jacksonville of the Southern League, when he hit .323/.393/.583 with 28 home runs and 146 RBI. This was no anomaly: Kapler has a career slugging percentage of .537 in 2,029 minor league at bats. But in the major leagues, despite playing the lion's share of his games in hitter-friendly parks in Texas and Boston, Kapler's slugging percentage is just .425.

Kapler did get off to a huge start after returning to the major leagues following a one-year retirement in 2007, hitting .283/.304/.566 in April 2008 for Milwaukee. He finished 2008 with a .301/.340/.498 line, excellent numbers. Still, at age 33, it is hard to imagine that Kapler will find the kind of consistent power hoped for when he was a top prospect with Detroit. And if he didn't attract the fawning Jewish women when he was a cover boy, how will he do it as a fourth outfielder?

Fortunately for Kapler, he is happily married, and he and his wife started the Gabe Kapler Foundation, dedicated to ending domestic abuse. He has far more important things to worry about than becoming a Jewish matinee idol.

## 5. Si Rosenthal
*Bats Left, Throws Left*
*Boston Red Sox, 1925–1926*

Si Rosenthal, like the center fielder ranked just below him, Harry Rosenberg, was an elite offensive player in the minor leagues, with a record eerily similar to Rosenberg's.

Rosenthal was five years older and made his major league debut five seasons sooner. He was a lefty, but he was born and raised on the right coast and collected most of his minor league hits in the East. He had 10 seasons with a batting average of .324 or higher but maxed out at just 21 home runs.

Rosenthal got a brief look at age 21–22, but he never returned to the big leagues, despite his minor league success.

To get a sense of the player Rosenthal was in his prime, look at his age-26 season—he hit .339 and slugged .475. Teammate Milt Stock, a longtime standout hitter in the National League, hit .307 with a .401 slugging. Granted, it was his age-36 season, but Stock was just two years removed from playing major league ball and hitting .328 for the Brooklyn Dodgers.

In the end, Rosenthal gets the edge due to the extra 348 at bats he logged in the major leagues. But neither hitter got to show what he could do at the highest level when he reached his prime.

### 6. Harry Rosenberg
*Bats Right, Throws Right*
*New York Giants, 1930*
These two center fielders really would have made the perfect platoon, and Rosenberg, like Rosenthal, certainly would have been an excellent addition to a major league club, given his minor league record.

Rosenberg was five pounds lighter than Rosenthal. He was a righty but made his name on the left coast. He had 12 full seasons with a batting average of .314 or higher but maxed out at just 16 home runs.

Much like Rosenthal, Rosenberg got just nine at bats at age 22, but he never returned to the big leagues, despite his minor league success.

Rosenberg had more games played and a higher career average than Rosenthal; of course, Rosenthal compiled his stats in more hitter-unfriendly leagues.

Rosenberg, in his age-27 season, outhit teammate and future major league All-Star Max West, .354 to .266, and outslugged him, .511 to .379. Granted, West was just 19, but even when West was 21 and Rosenberg was 29, each man hit .330 for the Mission Reds of the Pacific Coast League. A year later, West had an everyday job with the Boston Braves, while Rosenberg continued on in the PCL.

Ah, Rosenthal and Rosenberg—the platoon that might have been.

## 7. Ed Mensor

*Bats Both, Throws Right*
*Pittsburgh Pirates, 1912–1914*

According to *The Big Book of Jewish Baseball*, Ed Mensor was one of 17 children, and Mensor's father started a family baseball team. One can only imagine how psychologically damaging it would have been for a player on this team to get benched, or even platooned.

Mensor's nickname was "Midget," and he was listed at 5'6". Of course, that still places him nearly two feet taller than the only midget ever to play Major League Baseball, the 3'7" Eddie Gaedel. Amazingly, the three players nicknamed "Midget" nearly all overlapped their short careers, with Bill "Midget" Jones playing in 1911–1912 and Duke "Midget" Reilley playing in 1909.

Both Mensor and Jones took full advantage of their limited strike zone. Mensor's career batting average was .221, but his on-base percentage was .367. Jones put up a career .226 batting average and a .397 on-base percentage.

But Reilley had just a .258 on-base percentage to go with his .210 batting average, and drew just four walks. My suspicion is that Reilley was neither a midget nor, legally, a Duke. His full name was Alexander Aloysius Reilley, and as anyone would, he was looking for any nickname he could get.

## 8. Mark Gilbert

*Bats Both, Throws Right*
*Chicago White Sox, 1985*

Say this for Mark Gilbert—he went out on a high note. With everyday center fielder Darryl Boston out of the lineup, the White Sox called up the 28-year-old Gilbert to play all three outfield positions in July 1985, which he did in the course of a single week, logging time in left, center, and right.

Gilbert had hits in five of the six games he started, and scored runs in three of them. He had a hit and a walk July 25, a double on July 26, and a two-hit game on July 27 in the leadoff position.

So what does then–White Sox manager Tony LaRussa do? He plugs Luis Salazar, he of the .267 on-base percentage, into the leadoff position. Gilbert had four walks in his week in the big leagues. Salazar had 12 all year, in 327 at bats. And back to the minors he went.

## 9. Adam Greenberg

*Bats Left, Throws Right*
*Chicago Cubs, 2005*

If you rooted for Moonlight Graham in *Field of Dreams*, you really should root for Adam Greenberg. A top-flight collegiate center fielder at the University of North Carolina, he was selected in the ninth round of the 2002 draft by the Chicago Cubs.

Greenberg quickly climbed the ladder, showing above-average plate discipline everywhere he went and stealing bases at a very high percentage. His career minor league batting average is .268, but he has a .372 on-base percentage, and stole 112 bases in 151 attempts.

But on July 9, 2005, in his first major league at bat, on the first pitch, he was hit in the back of the head by a fastball. He didn't even get to run to first base. He suffered from postconcussive syndrome, and his 2005 season was lost. After a poor 2006 start in the minor leagues, the Cubs released him.

He had a solid 2007 with the AA Wichita Wranglers of the Kansas City Royals organization, hitting .266/.373/.428, but the Royals didn't keep him in 2008, and he played 2008 with the Arkansas Travelers of the Los Angeles Angels organization, hitting .271/.361/.347.

I'm not saying you need to root for injuries to all the Angels currently in the outfield. But at some point, justice needs to be served, and Adam Greenberg needs to get himself another major league at bat. And against a control pitcher.

| NAME | GAMES | AT BATS | OPS+ | WARP3 | Additional |
|------|-------|---------|------|-------|------------|
| 1. Elliott Maddox | 1029 | 2948 | 100 | 26.1 | Played 7 positions |
| 2. Lipman Pike | 425 | 1983 | 155 | 51.1 | First Jewish star |
| 3. Goody Rosen | 551 | 1916 | 111 | 21.0 | 1945 All-Star |
| 4. Gabe Kapler | 946 | 2654 | 92 | 20.3 | |
| 5. Si Rosenthal | 123 | 357 | 81 | −0.1 | 10 minor league years .324+ avg. |
| 6. Harry Rosenberg | 9 | 5 | −55 | −0.1 | 5 minor league years 200+ hits |
| 7. Ed Mensor | 127 | 244 | 88 | 1.7 | Career: 54 hits, 53 walks |
| 8. Mark Gilbert | 7 | 22 | 93 | 0.1 | |
| 9. Adam Greenberg | 1 | 0 | — | 0.0 | 1 game, 1 HBP |

**9**

# *Right Field*

Right field is the Jewish people's deepest position. If a baseball diamond were America, right field would be New York City. If a baseball team's roles were professional organizations, right field would be the American Bar Association. If all of baseball's positions were supermarkets, right field would be Zabar's.

Nineteen of baseball's Jews patrolled right field, and a large number of them excelled at the major league level. Cal Abrams and Art Shamsky were critical parts of championship teams, while Richie Scheinblum, in his one full season as a starter, was an All-Star.

Even the lesser right fielders like Mose Solomon and Micah Franklin put up huge home run totals. And one of the earliest right fielders, Jacob Pike, was one of baseball's first Jews.

*Shawn Green*

But far above the rest of the field is Shawn Green, one of the finest players in Jewish baseball history, though a premature decline kept him from seriously challenging for a spot in the Hall of Fame. Green put up three 40 home run seasons, second among Jewish players to Hank Greenberg's four. But Green also had four seasons with 20 or more steals, with a season high of 35—Greenberg's season high in steals was just 9.

Unfortunately for Green, his last great season was at age 29, and he didn't reach New York until age 33. So while Green's acquisition ended a 25-year Jewish player drought for the New York Mets, even the team's Jewish fans preferred Lastings Milledge, who famously wore a huge cross, in 2007. By 2008 Green was gone, and the Jewish fans much preferred the new guy, a man named Ryan Church. Religion goes only so far when your defense has deteriorated as much as Green's had.

Even with the fast decline, half a Hall of Fame career is nothing to airily dismiss.

## 1. Shawn Green

*Bats Left, Throws Left*
*Toronto Blue Jays, 1993–1999*
*Los Angeles Dodgers, 2000–2004*
*Arizona Diamondbacks, 2005–2006*
*New York Mets, 2006–2007*
*Baseball Prospectus 2003* on Shawn Green, as he entered his age-30 season: "Few players can hang with Green on the

field. . . . A durable player in top shape, it's a good bet you'll read a similar comment as he wraps up Year Six of his contract, in 2006."

*Baseball Prospectus 2007* on Shawn Green: "The Mets will only regret acquiring Shawn Green one time, and that's constantly. Since turning 30, Green has batted .277/.351/.458."

This is not to pick on *Prospectus*, in my opinion, the best of the baseball annuals. It was hard to imagine a player of Green's ability dropping off so quickly—that is what makes predicting the future in baseball so hard. As it is, the miasma of numbers makes the past and present pretty hard to interpret, too. But compare Green's numbers through age 29 to other Hall of Famers', and it is easy to see why so many people thought Green would be right there among the Greenberg/Koufax canon.

According to Baseball-Reference.com, his most similar batter through age 34 is Dave Winfield. He has two other Hall of Famers in his top 10, Carl Yastrzemski and Billy Williams.

Yaz vs. Green is particularly instructive. Through age 29, Green had 234 home runs in 4,324 at bats, Yaz had 202 home runs in 5,175 at bats. Each had three 40 home run seasons; Green had four 100 RBI seasons, Yaz three. Green's best adjusted OPS+ seasons were 154, 154, 143; Yaz's were 193, 170, 156. But Green's three best had come in his previous four seasons; Yaz had a 135 and a 119 mixed in.

Once adjusted for era, Yaz was the better player. By Prospectus's WARP3, Green was at 59.4 wins above replacement player through age 29, Yaz at 64.7. But it is remarkably close, considering that Yaz was a first-ballot Hall of Famer, and Green likely won't come close to enshrinement.

The other aspect that keeps Jewish players from earning the respect they deserve is that nearly every one of them had a below-average decline phase that started early. Here are some WARP3 figures for the finest Jewish players through age 29:

Shawn Green 59.4

Hank Greenberg 57.6

Sandy Koufax 56.4

Lou Boudreau 83

Al Rosen 40

And here is 30 and beyond:

Shawn Green 29.5

Hank Greenberg 19.4

Sandy Koufax 11.9

Lou Boudreau 27.1 (including 15.7 at age 30)

Al Rosen 13

Three of the five made the Hall anyway. But average declines might have pushed all five in—and gotten them into the larger discussion among the all-time greats.

## 2. Cal Abrams

*Bats Left, Throws Left*
*Brooklyn Dodgers, 1949–1952*
*Cincinnati Reds, 1952*

*Pittsburgh Pirates, 1953–1954*
*Baltimore Orioles, 1954–1955*
*Chicago White Sox, 1956*

Even biblical scholars speculate on just how much the words heeded in the Old Testament might have changed through the generations. Is it not possible, then, that the Jews were not the "Chosen People," as they are commonly referred to, but rather the "Choosy People"? Cal Abrams's ability to draw a walk is yet another example of a Jewish player with above-average plate discipline.

Abrams finished with a career batting average of .269 but an on-base percentage of .386. In a more enlightened statistical time, Abrams would have had regular outfield work, even with a below-average slugging percentage of .392. Really, as long as Billy Beane had a job, so would Cal Abrams. But Abrams never got 500 at bats in a season—in fact, in his career high of 1953, with 465, Abrams was traded midyear.

In fairness to the Dodgers, Abrams happened to come along at a time when Brooklyn simply didn't need out-fielders. Who would Abrams replace in Dodgerland, circa 1951—Duke Snider? Carl Furillo? Even the underrated Andy Pafko put up a .249/.350/.484 line with 30 home runs. But the Pirates and Orioles simply had no excuse not to play Abrams. If he'd gotten out of Brooklyn sooner, perhaps he'd have been viewed as a prospect. But there is little doubt Abrams was a better outfielder than many who got the chance to play every day.

Abrams also clearly identified with his Jewish roots—he wore the number 18, or *chai*, for much of his career—and his Dodger experience. According to his Associated Press obit, Abrams was buried in his Brooklyn Dodgers uniform. No word on whether or not Dodger Dogs were served at the *shiva*.

### 3. Art Shamsky

*Bats Left, Throws Left*
*Cincinnati Reds, 1965–1967*
*New York Mets, 1968–1971*
*Chicago Cubs, 1972*
*Oakland Athletics, 1972*

Art Shamsky provides a window into what a superstar Jewish baseball player would experience in New York. He played four seasons with the Mets, never getting more than 403 at bats in any season. Yet both Ray Romano and Jon Stewart named dogs after him. One can only speculate how many dogs Shamsky would have inspired had he played every day.

What is interesting about Shamsky's career is that he would have been an extremely useful everyday player, even with a tremendous platoon split. Shamsky's overall line looks ordinary by today's standards—.253/.330/.427— but he played in the most difficult hitting period since the deadball era, and 75 percent of his career was played in Shea Stadium, a pitcher's park. Just using Baseball-Reference.com's neutralizing feature, and his career line jumps to .263/.342/.443. His career OPS+ was 110—better than 12 of 18 outfielders in his own division in 1970, for instance.

Another quick point on Shamsky: Ron Swoboda is remembered as "the right fielder" on the 1969 Mets, due in large part to his game-saving catch in game 3 of the 1969 World Series. But Shamsky got 61 starts to Swoboda's 70 and outhit Swoboda .300/.375/.488 to .235/.326/.361. In WARP3, Shamsky nearly doubles Swoboda, 3.9 to 2.2. Pretty clearly, Art Shamsky was the team's best right fielder. Not a bad accomplishment for a team that won 100 games.

### 4. Richie Scheinblum
*Bats Both, Throws Right*
*Cleveland Indians, 1965, 1967–1969*
*Washington Senators, 1971*
*Kansas City Royals, 1972*
*Cincinnati Reds, 1973*
*California Angels, 1973–1974*
*Kansas City Royals, 1974*
*St. Louis Cardinals, 1974*

Like Shamsky, Richie Scheinblum was another above-average hitter whose raw totals were depressed by late '60s run environments. His final career line of .263/.343/.352 was good for a career OPS+ of 103 and in a neutral environment would be .287/.371/.388.

But two things appear to have held Scheinblum back. For one thing, he did not excel in short trials when the Indians desperately wanted to give him the right field job. With limited competition like Chuck Hinton and Vic Davalillo, Scheinblum hit .218 in 1968 and routinely hit "something like .180" in spring training each year, according to the March 29, 1969, issue of *The Sporting News*.

"For four years, I've been overawed," Scheinblum said in the same issue, "but not anymore."

Then he went out and hit .186 in 199 at bats.

Much of the time, something mental is used as an excuse by a player who simply can't hit big league pitching. But clearly, that wasn't the case for Scheinblum, who was a talented hitter. He went to the AAA Wichita Aeros of the American Association and hit .337/.424/.576 with 24 home runs in 1970. He improved on that star line with Wichita in 1971, hitting .388/.490/.725 (!) with another 25 home runs and just 26 strikeouts. He then returned to the majors with Washington in 1971 and hit .143.

Scheinblum finally got a full season in the major leagues in 1972, at age 29, and took full advantage. He flirted with a batting title all season, trailing eventual winner Rod Carew by just .317 to .316 as late as September 11, before a late-season slump dragged his season line down to .300/.383/.418, good for sixth in the American League. He struck out just 40 times, made the All-Star team, and was named AL Player of the Month in August.

However, Kansas City made him the main piece of a two-for-two trade that winter, to bring in Hal McRae. And

Scheinblum, whose fielding made him a prime candidate to DH, found himself in the National League for the debut of the new rule in 1973.

Scheinblum struggled in Cincinnati, hitting .222, and got shipped back to the American League, where he posted a .328/.417/.428 line for the Angels over 77 games in 1973. But he struggled through 1974 for three teams and headed to Japan, where he managed a .295/.349/.468 for the Hiroshima Toyo Carp, according to *Japan Daily*.

Anytime Scheinblum got the chance to settle into a full-time role, he hit. Unfortunately, teams often make player evaluations on small samples. They are statistically unreliable, and in Scheinblum's case, they probably cost him a career as a regular.

## 5. Herb Gorman
*Bats Left, Throws Left*
*St. Louis Cardinals, 1952*

Tragically, the record is incomplete for Herb Gorman. He was a masterful hitter, batting .351, .341, .310, and .305 from 1947 to 1950 in the Western and Pacific Coast Leagues, while posting slugging percentages of .516, .576, .473, and .470.

His numbers came down a bit in 1951–1952, though he still earned a call-up for the Cardinals in April 1952.

But after getting off to a 3-for-4 start in the 1953 season, Gorman suffered a heart attack on the field while playing for the San Diego Padres and soon thereafter died. He was 28 years old.

It is hard to imagine that a healthy Gorman wouldn't have returned to the major leagues.

## 6. Ruben Amaro Jr.

*Bats Right, Throws Right*
*California Angels, 1991*
*Philadelphia Phillies, 1992–1993*
*Cleveland Indians, 1994–1995*
*Philadelphia Phillies, 1996–1998*

Is it possible to quantify how value is added to a baseball player's career by having a Jewish mother? Ruben Amaro Jr., the product of a Jewish mother and a non-Jewish major league baseball player, may provide an answer.

Amaro Jr. and his father, Ruben Amaro Sr., both played in the major leagues. Both were similar hitters, though Amaro Sr. played shortstop, and Amaro Jr. was an outfielder. Amaro Sr. had 2,155 at bats for .234/.309/.292, good for an OPS+ of 71. Amaro Jr. hit .235/.310/.353, good for an OPS+ of 80. So pretty clearly, a Jewish mother added a significant amount of offense to Amaro Jr., primarily in power production.

Nine points of OPS+ is far from trivial. It is the difference between Willie Mays and Willie Stargell, Mike Piazza and John Kruk, Chuck Klein and J. D. Drew.

Let's hope, for his sake, that Amaro Jr. reliably called his mother to thank her for this gift.

## 7. Micah Franklin

*Bats Right, Throws Right*
*St. Louis Cardinals, 1997*

The Mets have a storied tradition of poor drafting, from Steve Chilcott over Reggie Jackson to Shawn Abner over everyone else. Micah Franklin, sadly, falls into that category as well. Franklin was selected by New York in the third round of the 1990 draft, ahead of fourth rounder Garret Anderson and fifth rounders Bret Boone and Ray Durham.

But the Mets gave up on Franklin after just two seasons, and he could have been useful in the organization. Franklin hit for power immediately upon leaving the Mets (at this point, virtually a cliché), putting up a .335 average and .534 slugging for Cincinnati's Pioneer League team. He went on to hit double figures in home runs 10 times in the minor leagues and hit 30 bombs for the Hokkaido Nippon Ham Fighters in 1999, which may be in violation of Jewish law.

Franklin even hit in his time with the Cardinals, posting a .324/.378/.500 line and a pair of home runs. But St. Louis elected not to bring him back, and he signed with the Chicago Cubs. He led the Iowa Cubs, and even the whole Pacific Coast League, in slugging percentage, putting up a .329/.437/.655 line. Unfortunately for Franklin, the Cubs had a right fielder that year, and Sammy Sosa put up a major league line of .308/.377/.647. Left fielder Henry Rodriguez added 31 home runs himself, and Franklin gave up on America and headed back to Japan.

By 2004 he posted a .284/.359/.537 line for AAA Tucson, but he couldn't get a call-up to the parent club, the Diamondbacks. At age 32, he called it a career.

## 8. Norm Miller

*Bats Left, Throws Right*
*Houston Astros, 1965–1973*
*Atlanta Braves, 1973–1974*

Add Miller to the list of hitters who were hurt by the pitching-dominated late '60s and the Astrodome—though his OPS+ was 94—so even in a neutral environment, his career line of .238/.323/.356 only rises to .258/.346/.382.

But Miller also was denied much development time. A Los Angeles kid, he was grabbed by the Angels in 1964 and excelled at Quad Cities in the A-level Midwest League, posting a .301/.448/.525 line. That was good enough to get plucked away by the Houston Astros, who promoted him late in 1965 after a .289/.402/.495 season for AA Amarillo of the Texas League.

Miller was 19, while teammates Larry Dierker, 18, and Rusty Staub and Joe Morgan, both 21, all got the chance to play major league baseball. But Miller never got the chance to play regularly—his season high in at bats was 409.

It must have felt to Miller like he got the majority of his career at bats on April 15, 1968. He played all 24 innings on Houston's 1–0 win over the Mets and led off the bottom of the 24th with a single, coming around to score the winning run. It was his first hit in 10 plate appearances.

A good comparison would be to Moses' 40 years in the desert, though Miller appears to come out ahead. After all, Moses didn't get to enter the Promised Land.

### 9. Fred Sington
*Bats Right, Throws Right*
*Washington Senators, 1934–1937*
*Brooklyn Dodgers, 1938–1939*

Fred Sington is another example of the rule that it is harder to hit major league pitching than to do nearly anything else in sports. A member of the college football Hall of Fame, Sington likely would have been a top draft pick of the NFL had the league been as prominent as it is today.

Instead, the man known as "Moose" found his way to baseball and used his power-hitting prowess to reach the major leagues. In 1932 he hit 35 home runs over 524 minor league at bats, and in 1934, he posted totals of 29 home runs, a .327 batting average, and a .579 slugging percentage for the Albany Crackers of the International League.

However, in 516 major league at bats over six seasons, Sington totaled just seven home runs. The 6'2", 215-pound Sington certainly had the strength to drive pitches out of the park, but not against major league pitching.

Sington went on to serve with distinction in World War II, rising to the level of lieutenant commander. This raises the question: is hitting a baseball even harder than waging war?

## 10. Dick Sharon

*Bats Right, Throws Right*
*Detroit Tigers, 1973–1974*
*San Diego Padres, 1975*

It is easy in retrospect to question the Pittsburgh Pirates' decision to draft Dick Sharon with the ninth overall pick in the 1968 draft, just two picks ahead of Greg Luzinski. Of course, Luzinski went on to hit 307 home runs, including 19 against the Pirates. Sharon fell 294 short of that total and never played for Pittsburgh.

But Sharon was known for both power and defense (certainly, Luzinski was known for defense, too, but more as Sammy's Restaurant is known for health food). Sharon's average, however, never made him a compelling choice for major league playing time; even in the minors, his average climbed above .255 once. In the big leagues, he struggled to reach even that—.218/.293/.355, good for a career OPS+ of 79.

He was a consistent plus at all three outfield positions and a threat to hit one out. But he simply didn't make enough contact to stick in the big leagues.

## 11. Milt Galatzer

*Bats Left, Throws Left*
*Cleveland Indians, 1933–1936*
*Cincinnati Reds, 1939*

Milt Galatzer was a skilled batter, though the extent to which his offensive value was tied to his batting average meant a couple of low averages in major league trials kept him from establishing a regular role in the big leagues.

Galatzer did not hit for power—he had 1 home run in 717 big league at bats, and his season high in any minor league season was 7, for the Class D Frederick Warriors in 1930. But he nearly never struck out: after 21 strikeouts in his first big league season, and 160 at bats, he fanned just 24 times over the next 547 at bats. So while his career line was just .268/.354/.326, clearly Galatzer was not overwhelmed by big league pitching.

Nine times in the minor leagues, Galatzer hit over .300 in a full season, and seven of those years his average was above .320. He hit for the Terre Haute Tots, he hit for the Toledo Mud Hens, he hit for the New Orleans Pelicans, he hit for the Indianapolis Indians. Had he gotten to play every day in the major leagues, chances are he'd have hit there, too.

But chances are, his use would have been limited as an everyday player. Galatzer did not steal bases (just 10 career steals in 22 attempts), and he really didn't get extra-base hits, either—only once did he accumulate 10 doubles in a season. But he'd have been a fine fourth outfielder. Instead, he played until 1946, with the obvious interruption to serve his country, and was a minor league Brett Butler.

## 12. Mose Solomon
*Bats Left, Throws Left*
*New York Giants, 1923*

Nobody had a better nickname in major league history than Mose "the Rabbi of Swat" Solomon. And he earned it with one of the finest individual seasons any minor leaguer had.

In 1923, playing for the Hutchinson, Kansas, Wheat Shockers of the Class C Southwestern League, Solomon hit .421 with 49 home runs, slugging .833 in the process.

It's a long way from Class C to the majors, but the New York Giants snapped him up, earning front-page stories in *The Sporting News* in consecutive weeks.

September 6, 1923: Headlined "Dick Kinsella Finds That $100,000 Jew" (Kinsella was a scout for the Giants), an article touted Solomon as a player who would "become as popular at the Polo Grounds as Babe Ruth has been with followers of the Yankees in New York." Rest assured, the Giants didn't pay $100,000 for Solomon; they merely thought he'd be worth that much to the team.

Any investment that increases 10-fold in value in a week is pretty impressive, so the September 13, 1923, headline "Worth Million to Giants?" simply reinforced the Solomon hype. Asserting that there were "more Jews in New York than in all of Palestine," the article indicated this was Solomon's new worth to the Giants. Solomon was also touted for his fighting skills, which likely came in handy as a Jew playing baseball in 1923 Kansas. Indeed, *The Sporting News* reported that word soon went around the league to "lay off the big Jew," which is respectful in some ways, certainly the best he could have hoped for from opponents. He was known as the "Hutchinson Jew"—which I'm sure, by itself, was an identifier.

Solomon managed a .375 average in 8 at bats with the 1923 Giants, but his primary position, first base, was manned by the Hall of Famer George Kelly, with fellow Hall of Famer Bill Terry in wait. He was sent to the minors for more seasoning, but at higher levels, his power disappeared. In 1925, playing for the Hartford/Albany Senators of the AA Eastern League, he hit just 2 home runs in 511 at bats. That was a far cry from 49.

A closer examination of Hutchinson's totals indicates that the Wheat Shockers might have played in a tremendous hitter's park. Solomon led the team with 49 home runs, but he had teammates with 35 and 21, while his 15 triples made him one of four Hutchinson players to reach double figures in three-baggers.

But that magical season of 1923, Solomon even pitched two games for the Wheat Shockers. He allowed 9 runs in 11 innings and went 2–0.

Hutchinson, Kansas, was no place for pitchers' duels.

### 13. Brian Kowitz
*Bats Left, Throws Left*
*Atlanta Braves, 1995*
Brian Kowitz was a legitimately great college player for Clemson University. He hit .403, had a 37-game hitting streak,

and made the all-ACC first team, as well as *Baseball America*'s second-team All America.

Atlanta made Kowitz, a bit on the small side at 5'10", 180 pounds, its ninth-round pick in the 1990 draft, grabbing him ahead of players like Fernando Vina, Tony Graffanino, and Rusty Greer. Kowitz started slowly in professional ball, largely due to a promotion from rookie ball straight to AA, but when repeating the high-A Carolina League, he hit .301 with a .429 on-base percentage for the Durham Bulls, earning him promotions to AA and then AAA in rapid succession.

He reached his apex as a prospect in 1994, putting up a .300/.357/.444 line for AAA Richmond, stealing 22 bases, and leading his team to the International League title. He capped the year with an appearance as "utility player/coach" in *Major League II*. I like to think he comes in to replace Pedro Serrano for defense in a bunch of double-switch scenes that got cut out of the final version, though this is pure speculation on my part.

Kowitz's average dropped to .280 and his slugging to .365 for Richmond in 1995, though he did get a shot to replace the injured David Justice midyear. But he hit just .167/.259/.208 in 24 at bats and never saw big league action again.

### 14. Adam Stern
*Bats Left, Throws Right*
*Boston Red Sox, 2005–2006*
*Baltimore Orioles, 2007*

It was Adam Stern's rotten luck to play for the Boston Red Sox in the two seasons between their two recent World Series victories. Fellow Jewish players Gabe Kapler got to experience one and Kevin Youkilis got to experience both. But Stern was left out in the cold.

Stern was picked up by Atlanta in the third round of the 2001 draft, with the 105th overall pick (Ryan Howard went 140th). Stern never played for Atlanta, as he was a Rule V draft pick by Boston after Stern posted a stellar AA season for Greenville, hitting .322 with a .480 slugging percentage. (The Rule V draft allows major league teams to select anyone not on another team's 40-man roster, with the proviso that the team must keep the player on the major league team all season or offer the player back to his original team.)

After Stern returned to the minors, he had another superlative season, posting a .321/.385/.494 line. But in 2006 that line came way down, to .258/.300/.388. Dealt to Baltimore, he hit .270/.326/.360. In 2008 his line for AAA Norfolk was just .221/.254/.303, leaving this onetime prospect with the likelihood of never reaching the big leagues again.

The biggest tragedy of all in this is that Stern is Canadian, and had a Canadian-Jewish player become a star, there's a good chance announcers could have applauded his "Can-Jew Spirit." But now? They may never get the chance.

### 15. Max Rosenfeld
*Bats Right, Throws Right*
*Brooklyn Dodgers, 1931–1933*

While the "Brooklyn Dodgers as America" theme really took hold when Jackie Robinson broke the color barrier in 1947, the January 29, 1931, edition of *The Sporting News* described the team as "A Team of All Nations" in a page 1 headline. Max Rosenfeld and Alta Cohen made up the Jewish contingent, while "Frank [Lefty] O'Doul in left is very Irish."

Sadly for the Jews, neither Rosenfeld nor Cohen stuck, though Rosenfeld did have a strong 1932—.359/.359/.590 in 39 at bats. Instead, Rosenfeld settled into a long career in the high minors, hitting .260 to .280, slugging .360 to .380, and eventually landing the player/manager's job with the Miami Beach Flamingos.

While his religion couldn't have been a drawback for the good people of Miami Beach, he earned his money there—he hit .341 in 1940, and in the winter of 1945, as the Florida International League prepared to resume for the 1946 season, he even served as temporary chairman of the circuit.

### 16. Sam Mayer
*Bats Right, Throws Right*
*Washington Senators, 1915*
Sam Mayer played respectably well in his September 1915 call-up with the Washington Senators, posting a .241/.333/.345 line, which was good enough in 1915 terms for an OPS+ of 101.

And certainly one can look favorably upon his 18-year

minor league career. He hit early and late, posting a .307 batting average and .467 slugging percentage for the Fulton Colonels of the Kentucky-Illinois-Tennessee League and a .319 batting average and .398 slugging percentage for the Pittsfield Hillies of the Eastern League, playing in beautiful Wahconah Park.

But I am most intrigued that the brother of Erskine Mayer, the hugely successful pitcher, tried his hand at the craft himself. For Savannah of the South Atlantic League in 1913–1914, he pitched a total of 87 innings, allowed 29 runs, and walked just 37. If all the runs were earned, his ERA was still just 2.97. Six years later, he pitched another seven innings for Atlanta of the Southern Association, allowed just one run, and picked up the victory.

In all, he was 7–3 in his minor league pitching career. So what stopped him from pitching? Did he not want to be caught in his brother's shadow? Was his hitting so good that teams didn't want to use him merely on the mound? There's an untold story in that career stat line.

### 17. Sam Fuld
*Bats Left, Throws Left*
*Chicago Cubs, 2007*
Time is running out for Fuld, a very similar player to Max Rosenfeld. The New Hampshire High School Player of the Year in 2000 and standout outfielder for Stanford, Fuld has continued to hit for a high average, steal some bases, and

field his position well at every level for the Cubs. But so far, he's gotten very little chance to play.

Fuld repeated AA and AAA in 2008, after posting a .287/.376/.395 line between AA and AAA in 2007. In AA, he hit .271/.366/.381; in AAA, just .222/.310/.317.

John Sickels, the dean of all prospect evaluators, wrote of Fuld in *The Prospect Book 2008*: "I think he would be an excellent fourth outfielder, due to his speed, defense, on-base ability, and hustle."

But this was Fuld's age-26 season. Too much longer, and prospects tend to get relabeled as organizational soldiers and lose their chance. He could be the Jewish Endy Chavez or, if he gets lucky, the Jewish Juan Pierre. Hopefully, it will happen soon; his skills once again manifested themselves at AA and AAA. All he needs is a shot.

### 18. Nate Berkenstock

*Bats Unknown, Throws Unknown*
*Philadelphia Athletics, 1871*

According to Baseball-Reference.com's Bullpen, the oldest known professional baseball player, Nate Berkenstock, was born in 1831. By 1871 he'd helped to form the Philadelphia Athletics, but his playing days were over. Then, just prior to the last game of the season—the championship game!—right fielder Count Sensenderfer had injured his knee, and Berkenstock stepped in, the logical choice given Philadelphia's apparent 10-letter minimum for right fielder last names.

Berkenstock was 0-for-4 with three strikeouts, but he also made three putouts in right, including the final one, as Philadelphia defeated Chicago, 4–1, to win the National Association title.

### 19. Jacob Pike

*Bats Left, Throws Left*
*Hartford Dark Blues, 1877*

Pike was the older brother of early baseball star Lipman Pike. Accounts vary on such things as whether his name was Jacob or Israel—either way, that's a name for a Jewish ballplayer. Lipman Pike? Did you ever meet a Jew named Lipman? And last name doesn't count.

Regardless, according to Peter Morris of the SABR Biography Project, we know for sure that Pike became a haberdasher. We are merely reasonably sure that he is the same Pike who earned one hit in four at bats for the Hartford Dark Blues, who were a member of the National League.

Rest assured, in my forthcoming sequel, *The Haberdasher Talmud*, this Pike will rank much higher.

| NAME | GAMES | AT BATS | OPS+ | WARP3 | Additional |
|------|-------|---------|------|-------|------------|
| 1. Shawn Green | 1951 | 7082 | 120 | 82.9 | 2001: 49 HR in pitcher's park |
| 2. Cal Abrams | 567 | 1611 | 112 | 14.2 | .386 career OBP |
| 3. Art Shamsky | 665 | 1686 | 110 | 15.6 | |
| 4. Richie Scheinblum | 462 | 1218 | 103 | 6.9 | 1972 All-Star |
| 5. Herb Gorman | 1 | 1 | –100 | 0.0 | Minor league doubles machine |

| NAME | GAMES | AT BATS | OPS+ | WARP3 | Additional |
|---|---|---|---|---|---|
| 6. Ruben Amaro Jr. | 485 | 927 | 80 | 5.1 | |
| 7. Micah Franklin | 17 | 34 | 129 | 0.4 | MLB missed the boat on him |
| 8. Norm Miller | 540 | 1364 | 94 | 5.8 | |
| 9. Fred Sington | 181 | 516 | 103 | 4.2 | |
| 10. Dick Sharon | 242 | 467 | 79 | 1.9 | |
| 11. Milt Galatzer | 251 | 717 | 75 | 1.1 | |
| 12. Mose Solomon | 2 | 8 | 130 | 0.1 | 49 HR in 1923 minors |
| 13. Brian Kowitz | 10 | 24 | 24 | −0.3 | |
| 14. Adam Stern | 48 | 35 | 14 | −0.1 | |
| 15. Max Rosenfeld | 42 | 57 | 115 | 0.4 | |
| 16. Sam Mayer | 11 | 29 | 101 | 0.3 | |
| 17. Sam Fuld | 14 | 6 | −4 | 0.3 | Plus defense, plus eye |
| 18. Nate Berkenstock | 1 | 4 | −100 | 0.0 | Would be 178 years old in 2009 |
| 19. Jacob Pike | 1 | 4 | 65 | −0.2 | |

# 10

## Left-Handed Starters

Pretty much everyone knows this discussion starts and ends with Sandy Koufax, though due to a significantly longer career, Ken Holtzman holds the record for most wins by a Jewish starting pitcher over Koufax, 174–165. Of course, Holtzman's career record is 174–150; Koufax's is 165–87.

Based on WARP3, Koufax tops Holtzman, 68.3 to 51.6, meaning that, despite three extra seasons for Holtzman, Koufax's career was about 25 percent more valuable. This is not a knock on Holtzman, a very good pitcher; Koufax was simply that good.

To me, the saddest part about Sandy Koufax, who retired after his age-30 season due to arthritis in his elbow, is that while the injury ended his career, it hadn't ended his effectiveness. In fact, he'd become a better pitcher as he aged, and 1966, his final season, was arguably his best. I've also heard

*Sandy Koufax*

it argued that his problem could easily have been fixed with minor surgery today.

Keep in mind also that pitching numbers only got better in 1967–1968—merely by pitching to age 32, Koufax was a near lock for over 200 wins. Bob Gibson, who was the same age as Koufax, pitched to a 2.44 ERA in 1966 but 1.12 in 1968. Would Koufax have put up a sub-1.00 ERA in 1968? It certainly seems possible.

## 1. Sandy Koufax

*Bats Right, Throws Left*
*Brooklyn Dodgers, 1955–1957*
*Los Angeles Dodgers, 1958–1966*

In his updated *Historical Baseball Abstract*, Bill James argues, correctly, that Sandy Koufax posted an ERA roughly twice as high on the road as he did at Dodger Stadium, a notorious pitcher's park—57–15, 1.37 ERA at home; 54–19, 2.57 ERA on the road.

But what is missed in this analysis is that Koufax got better as he aged away from Dodger Stadium; indeed, he became nearly as elite a pitcher on the road as at home by age 30. His home ERAs were static, and ridiculous—1.75, 1.38, 0.85, 1.38, 1.52. But away, watch the progression: 3.53, 2.31, 2.93, 2.72, 1.96. By 1966 his road ERA was within half a run of his home ERA. Batting average against was .202 at home, .207 on the road, a negligible difference. And his strikeout rate was actually higher on the road (157 in 151²/₃ innings) than at home (160 in 171¹/₃ innings).

So while James doesn't argue that Koufax was a Dodger Stadium creation, others have, and incorrectly. Let's stack up Koufax's 1966 against the 2007 Cy Young winners—but give Koufax the benefit of just his road work.

Road Koufax, 1966: 151 IP, 14–4 record, 1.96 ERA, 32 BB, 157 K

Jake Peavy, 2007: 223 IP, 19–6 record, 2.54 ERA, 68 BB, 240 K

C. C. Sabathia, 2007: 241 IP, 19–7 record, 3.21 ERA, 37 BB, 209 K

While Koufax's win total might have hurt him, voters would have been hard-pressed to vote for either Peavy or Sabathia over Road Koufax.

Now, this obviously fails to take era into account. But I have strong suspicions that at the extreme in performance represented by Koufax, era adjustments are unfair. Obviously, fewer runs were scored in the 1962–1966 era than, for instance, the five-year period of dominance by Pedro Martinez, 1999–2003. Beyond a certain point, though, I believe it is impossible for pitchers to avoid giving up runs. Defense, no matter the offensive period, is ultimately finite, and grounders will find holes, fly balls will find gaps or leave the park entirely. Unless a pitcher is striking out 400 men a season with a minimum of walks (and Koufax came as close as anyone since 1900 to doing so, striking out 382 in 1965 against just 71 walks), there is a floor for a pitcher's ERA, and it isn't 0.00.

Adjusting ERA for era and park, as the terrific stat ERA+

(which adjusts a raw ERA for park and era and expresses it relative to league average—100 being average, and 105, for instance, 5 percent better than league average) does, is a fine shorthand for pitcher evaluation. I simply suspect it fails, on the extreme here, to evaluate the difference between Koufax's 190 in 1966 and Martinez's 291 in 2000.

One other note: Koufax won an MVP in 1963 but finished second in 1965 to Willie Mays, and in 1966 to Roberto Clemente. A win both seasons would have made him the only pitcher to be a three-time winner, and he'd have joined Hank Greenberg as a Jewish player with multiple MVPs.

But while Mays's 1965 edges Koufax's in WARP3, 13.9 to 10.3, Koufax's 1966 WARP3 beats out the winner's, Roberto Clemente's, 11.9 to 10.9. Plus, the Dodgers finished first that season; the Pirates were third. Even head-to-head, Koufax won the battle, holding Clemente to a .231 bating average in 13 at bats. This is a puzzling choice, to say the least.

Think Koufax was valuable? The 1966 Dodgers finished 95–67. The 1967 Dodgers, sans Koufax, came in at 73–89. Bill Singer, his replacement in the rotation, put up a 12–8, 2.64 ERA season, good for an ERA+ of 116. And Don Drysdale, who had struggled in 1966, improved his performance in 1967 from a 96 ERA+ to 112. Still, the Dodgers won 22 fewer games. Koufax was that good.

## 2. Ken Holtzman
*Bats Right, Throws Left*
*Chicago Cubs, 1965–1971*

*Oakland Athletics, 1972–1975*
*Baltimore Orioles, 1976*
*New York Yankees, 1976–1978*
*Chicago Cubs, 1978–1979*

Ken Holtzman was a very good major league pitcher. There are conventional ways of measuring this—the 174 wins, the career ERA+ of 105, the pair of no-hitters. But what is striking about Holtzman is the way he seemed to raise his game, hit another level of ability. While it is hard to quantify clutch performance, due to sample size, there are plenty of exhibits in Holtzman's career.

Take 1969, when he was serving in the military, yet still could return to the Cubs to pitch weekend games. A disruption in routine like that would adversely affect most pitchers. But Holtzman pitched 261 1/3 innings of 113 ERA+ baseball, winning 17 games.

His postseason numbers also far surpass his regular season stats—in 13 postseason games, 12 starts, he went 6-1 with a 2.30 ERA in 70 innings. But it doesn't even end there—a career .163 hitter, Holtzman hit .308/.357/.769 in 13 postseason at bats, with three doubles.

And there's more. His second lowest ERA by month was September. In his career, hitters had a batting average against of .255, but with runners in scoring position, it dropped to .244 (usually, this number goes up). Even with the bases loaded, the number stood at .256, with just two grand slams given up in 184 plate appearances—a home run rate half of his overall career mark.

And take September 25, 1966, in a late-season game between the Cubs and Dodgers. It meant nothing in the standings (the Cubs were firmly ensconced in eighth place), but for Holtzman, going up against Sandy Koufax, the game had to have extra meaning.

Holtzman took a no-hitter into the ninth, and bested Koufax, 2–1. It was Sandy's final regular-season loss in the major leagues—he won his final two decisions, then went 1–1 in the 1966 World Series—and he allowed just four hits, striking out five. But Holtzman allowed two hits and struck out eight.

It didn't quite turn out to be a changing of the guard. Holtzman simply didn't measure up to Koufax, though in fairness, few pitchers did. But again, in a big spot, this time for Jewish supremacy, Holtzman came up big. Is he a clutch pitcher? There's too much evidence to ignore.

### 3. Dave Roberts
*Bats Left, Throws Left*
*San Diego Padres, 1969–1971*
*Houston Astros, 1972–1975*
*Detroit Tigers, 1976–1977*
*Chicago Cubs, 1977–1978*
*Pittsburgh Pirates, 1979–1980*
*Seattle Mariners, 1980*
*New York Mets, 1981*

A far better pitcher than his career record of 103–125 showed, Dave Roberts was health challenged. But he still piled up

2,099 innings of 3.78 ERA ball, good for a career ERA+ mark of 97, which is just about average for a starter (100 is true average, but relievers tend to have a higher ERA+).

When Roberts was healthy, however, he was much better than average. In his five seasons from 1970 to 1974, his average ERA+ was around 113. For context, Nolan Ryan's career ERA+ was 111.

A mark of how good a healthy Roberts was came in 1979, when the Pittsburgh Pirates acquired him midyear to use him as a swing man. Roberts pitched 38 1/3 innings of 121 ERA+ ball for Pittsburgh as the Pirates won the World Series.

It was the only time Roberts pitched for a team that won more than 84 games. Five seasons, his teams lost 97 games or more, and his final team, the 1981 Mets, were on pace to reach 97 losses, were it not for the strike. A little better luck with his rosters, and Roberts, who trails Steve Stone for third place among wins by Jewish pitchers, would have finished considerably ahead of him.

### 4. Ross Baumgarten
*Chicago White Sox, 1978–1981*
*Pittsburgh Pirates, 1982*

There are few better examples of how meaningless won-loss records are for a pitcher than Ross Baumgarten's 1980 season.

Baumgarten shot through the Chicago White Sox system after being taken in the 20th round of the 1977 draft. His

minor league career included a 9–1, 1.82 ERA stop at Apple-
ton of the Midwest League, but he pitched very well at each
level. After 23 innings at the major league level in 1978, he
earned a rotation spot in 1979 and went 13–8 with a 3.54
ERA. His future seemed secure.

But in 1980, Baumgarten went 2–12. His ERA was actually
lower than in 1978, 3.44. His walk rate went down, his strikeout rate went up. He lost games 1–0, 3–1, 3–2, and 3–2 again.
He got no-decisions in another five games where he threw
quality starts, pitching 34²/₃ innings of 1.81 ERA baseball in
those five games. Teammate La Marr Hoyt had an ERA more
than a run higher, and his record was 9–3.

A side note: Baumgarten pitched a one-hitter in one of his
only two victories that season, on July 2. His team got him
only one run. And Rod Carew, supposed friend to the Jews,
because he married a Jewish woman and raised his kids in
the faith, got the hit off Baumgarten. Thanks a lot, Rod. I
guess your admirable Jewish charitable work didn't include
the Ross Baumgarten No-Hitter Foundation.

The loss total undoubtedly put Baumgarten on a short
leash, and after a difficult 1981, he was traded to Pittsburgh,
where a deserved 0–5 start ended his major league career.
But his career 22–36 mark is unjustified. Baseball-Refer-
ence.com has his neutralized won-loss record at 31–27.

In reality, had he posted a second double-digit-win season,
he'd likely have gotten plenty of chances to keep pitching, instead of being viewed, unfairly, as a fluke. That win number,
with a luckier 1980, would have been a lot higher.

## 5. Lefty Weinert

*Bats Left, Throws Left*
*Philadelphia Phillies, 1919–1924*
*Chicago Cubs, 1927–1928*
*New York Yankees, 1931*

Lefty Weinert began as very sought-after property—he was the subject of a dispute between the Phillies, who wanted to call him up, and the Reading Coal Barons, who wanted to keep him. He was just 17 and had posted a 6–15 record and 4.80 ERA in the International League. For the pitching-starved Phils, a youngster with talent, and a hometown boy, must have been too good to pass up. The gentlemen's agreement was held up, and Weinert became a Phillie.

There, he pitched for some absolutely putrid baseball teams. The 1920 Phils went 62–91; that was their high-water mark while Weinert was a Phillie. He spent 1922 in the rotation, with a respectable 8–11, 3.40 ERA showing, good for an ERA+ of 136. The ERA placed him seventh in the National League—adjusting for park and era pushed him to second in the NL that year. That he did this at age 20 was remarkable.

The 1923 season did not go as well. The record was 4–17, the ERA 5.42. In May 1924, Weinert was optioned to Los Angeles of the Pacific Coast League, where he posted a 2–3 record, 5.29 ERA.

Unfortunately, Weinert's 1925 and 1926 seasons appear lost to history. There is no major or minor league record that I know of, and when *The Sporting News* next mentions him, in the September 8, 1927, issue, only his 1927 pitch-

ing is mentioned. It certainly deserved notice, of course—
he went 17–12 with a 3.14 ERA in the notoriously hitter-
friendly PCL, for Mission.

The performance earned him 15 games, including another 4 starts, for the 1927–1928 Chicago Cubs. Unfortunately, the magic wore off, as he posted ERAs of 4.58 and
5.29 for Chicago.

An 18-win, 3.00 ERA season for the A-level Memphis
Chickasaws in 1929 and a 16-win, 3.63 ERA campaign for
the AA Louisville Colonels in 1930 earned Weinert a third
shot, with the 1931 New York Yankees. Now 29, Weinert
struck out a hitter per inning. But his ERA in those 24 frames
was 6.20, and by July, according to the July 9, 1931, issue of
*The Sporting News*, "[Yankees manager Joe] McCarthy clung
to him, always hoping that he would flash big league stuff,
but finally decided that he would help Louisville more than
[New York owner] Colonel [Jacob] Ruppert's club." *The
Sporting News* did note that Weinert "seemed to be pursued
by considerable hard luck."

Three chances to make good in the major leagues is pretty
lucky, especially at that time. Weinert posted another three
double-digit win totals in the minor leagues from 1932 to
1934. Still, 1922 was Weinert's *Citizen Kane*—by the '30s, he
was making commercials for frozen peas.

### 6. Harry Kane
*Bats Left, Throws Left*
*St. Louis Browns, 1902*

*Detroit Tigers, 1903*
*Philadelphia Phillies, 1905–1906*
While Harry Kane pitched for 13 years, for the Wichita Falls Drillers to the Hugo Hugoites, the Williamsport Millionaires to the Springfield Midgets, he had his greatest success with Savannah of the Southern Association in 1905–1906, winning 22 games in 1905, 17 wins the following year.

For the man born Harry Cohen, I can only wonder how many fans were aware of his religion, and how much the people of Savannah cared as he anchored the team's staff. Anti-Semitism didn't stop him from big league success, however—86 innings of 62 ERA+ pitching did.

### 7. Bill Cristall

*Bats Left, Throws Left*
*Cleveland Blues, 1901*
Don't get me started on Bill Cristall, the Jodie Dallas of Ukrainian baseball players, who had a simply marvelous 18-year career in the minor leagues.

But for the 1901 Cleveland Blues, Bill Cristall was not the Candyman. (That was, clearly, their first baseman, Candy LaChance.) His appearances were sweet for the opposition, however, with a 4.74 ERA, 1–5 record, and ERA+ of 73—he was no Miracle Max.

The Blues were no masochists; they forgot Cristall. But Cristall won 10 or more games 6 times in the next 16 minor league seasons, and despite standing just 5'7", played "My

Giant" to the New York State Capital region, logging seasons for Albany, Schenectady, and Troy.

After 700 Sundays as a player, Cristall eventually moved on to managing, but after starting 1919 in charge of the Bay City Wolves of the Michigan-Ontario League, he was replaced midyear. I guess nobody told Wolves management that if you rush a miracle man, you get rotten miracles.

| NAME | GAMES | INNINGS | ERA+ | W-L | Additional |
|------|-------|---------|------|-----|------------|
| 1. Sandy Koufax | 397 | 2324.3 | 131 | 165–87 | 3 Cy Youngs |
| 2. Ken Holtzman | 451 | 2867.3 | 105 | 174–150 | 2 no-hitters |
| 3. Dave Roberts | 445 | 2099 | 97 | 103–125 | |
| 4. Ross Baumgarten | 90 | 495.3 | 100 | 22–36 | 13 wins in 1979 |
| 5. Lefty Weinert | 131 | 437 | 96 | 18–33 | |
| 6. Harry Kane | 15 | 86 | 62 | 2–7 | |
| 7. Bill Cristall | 6 | 48.3 | 73 | 1–5 | |

# 11

# *Right-Handed Starters*

There are no Sandy Koufax types among the 12 right-handed Jewish starters in baseball history, but a majority of these pitchers would be a good fit in nearly any rotation.

What is astounding is how close the top few are to one another. Check out the top righties, as ranked by ERA+:

1. Barney Pelty 100
2. Erskine Mayer 99
3. Steve Stone 98
4. Saul Rogovin 96
5. Jason Marquis 96
6. Barry Latman 94

Ultimately, Pelty gets the nod for a number of reasons that extend beyond the tiny edge in ERA+. Pelty holds the innings edge over his rivals for the top spot with 1,908 IP.

*Barney Pelty*

But while this is an imperfect means of judging him against his more modern rivals, it allows us to see a 25 percent cushion over Erskine Mayer, who pitched in a similar time.

Pelty had four full seasons with an ERA+ of better than 100, including a 163, 120, and 114. Marquis's top season was 128, though among seasons he was primarily a starter, that high ERA+ is just 115. For Steve Stone, his top season was a 123, with only one other full starting season above 100, at 106.

Nor does it hurt that Pelty had the finest Jewish-themed baseball nickname this side of the Rabbi of Swat—Pelty was known as "the Yiddish Curver." Figure also that Pelty played on poor teams (until his final half-season in Washington, none of his teams finished higher than fourth place). It is fair to surmise that his won-loss record would have been much better (Baseball-Reference.com adjusts his 92–117 to average teams and parks, putting it at a far more impressive 125–84), and teams that poor usually have below-average fielding teams. Such fielding doesn't get fully captured by ERA, as the plays fielders don't come close to are just as rough on pitchers as those they boot away.

Through all of that, Barney Pelty still stands as the finest Jewish right-handed pitcher of all time.

### 1. Barney Pelty

*Bats Right, Throws Right*
*St. Louis Browns, 1902–1912*
*Washington Senators, 1912*

Due to the gaudy won-loss total in his finest season, Steve

Stone generally gets the edge when people name the finest right-handed pitcher. But a close comparison between Stone's 1980 and Pelty's 1906 shows Pelty's to be the far superior season.

Stone did register a 25–7 mark, while Pelty came in at 16–11. But Stone pitched for a 100–62 Orioles team, Pelty for the 76–73 Browns (who went on to become the Orioles). Stone received slightly more than 5.5 runs per game in his starts, 204 runs over 37 starts. Pelty, it is safe to say, received far less than that—he started 30 of St. Louis's 149 games, but the Browns scored 558 runs all season.

Pelty's ERA was 1.59; Stone's, 3.25. And even once accounting for park and era, Pelty's ERA+ was 163, while Stone's was 123.

Stone had a great season. But Pelty had a far greater season—and a better career around it, too.

Incidentally, had Pelty's neutralized 125–84 record stood, he'd have had a .598 career winning percentage—good for 117th all time, and just ahead of Warren Spahn and Curt Schilling.

## 2. Erskine Mayer

*Bats Right, Throws Right*
*Philadelphia Phillies, 1912–1918*
*Pittsburgh Pirates, 1918–1919*
*Chicago White Sox, 1919*

Erskine Mayer was a very capable number two starter on the 1915 Phillies, a team that went to the World Series. But keep in mind, he had a season that would have made him an ace on many other pennant winners. The number one starter was the great Grover Cleveland Alexander, who had his finest season—31–10, 1.22 ERA.

Mayer was a Southern Jew from Atlanta, the son of musicians. He drew the attention of scouts with a 15–2 record for the Fayetteville Highlanders of the Class D Eastern Carolina League. The Phils snapped him up in 1912, and by 1913 he was a fixture on the Philadelphia staff, posting a 9–9 record in 170 1/3 innings of 3.11 ERA (107 ERA+) pitching.

In 1914 he was nearly the equal of the great Alexander. Mayer posted a 21–19 record, 2.58 ERA, while Alexander was at 27–15, 2.38 ERA. Then came his huge season.

It appears injuries slowed Mayer over the remainder of his career. He'd be effective, but in shorter and shorter bursts. By 1919 he had posted an 8.37 ERA for the White Sox—ironic, since he was one of the White Sox who *wasn't* throwing games.

Added to Mayer's ledger, incidentally, is his hitting—a career line of .185/.234/.252 with a pair of home runs is good for a pitcher in any time, but Mayer was hitting in the deadball era.

Mayer and Stone, incidentally, are about as close as any two rated players in this book. Mayer posted an ERA+ of 99 in his career, just ahead of Stone's 98. However, Stone pitched 1,788 1/3 innings; Mayer pitched 1,427.

So why the edge for Mayer? In all, Mayer had five seasons of above-average production—ERA+ marks over a full season of 116, 113, 110, 107, and 102. Stone had just three such seasons, posting 123, 118, and 106. In a close race, I'll take the guy who had above-average seasons five times in 8 years over the one who did so three times in 11 years.

In all, Mayer is unjustly forgotten by most baseball fans, apparently not a new experience for him. As the September 9, 1915, issue of *The Sporting News* reports of Mayer: "It may be he thought he should have more credit for it and that there should be a little more said about Mayer and less about Alexander. Looking over that record, we incline to think along the same lines."

Hollywood disagreed—and Ronald Reagan played Alexander in 1952's *The Winning Team*, not Mayer.

### 3. Steve Stone

*Bats Right, Throws Right*
*San Francisco Giants, 1971–1972*
*Chicago White Sox, 1973*
*Chicago Cubs, 1974–1976*
*Chicago White Sox, 1977–1978*
*Baltimore Orioles, 1979–1981*

Steve Stone's career started and ended with his curveball.

According to *The Big Book of Jewish Baseball*, Stone decided to throw mostly curveballs in 1980, though he knew such a choice would ruin his arm, which had been sore for the better part of eight years. The results were huge—a 25–7 record, 3.25 ERA. It was easily the best season of his career, winning percentage wise, and many point to it as a fluke season.

But this severely underrates how good a healthy Stone could be. Back in 1971, when he was a rookie starter for the San Francisco Giants, he was heralded as "the most promising young pitcher we've had since Juan Marichal came up" in the May 1, 1971, edition of *The Sporting News.* The one speaking was Giants coach Larry Jansen, an excellent pitcher in his own right.

In that same article, what did Stone credit his success to? "I began getting my curve over the plate last year," he said. "That's the main reason I improved enough to merit a chance up here."

By 1972 he had posted just a 6–8 record but a 2.98 ERA, good for an ERA+ of 118. Injuries may have taken their toll in between, but Stone and his curveball were no fluke.

## 4. Jason Marquis

*Bats Right, Throws Right*
*Atlanta Braves, 2000–2003*
*St. Louis Cardinals, 2004–2006*
*Chicago Cubs, 2007–*

While Jason Marquis is unlikely to post a season on par with the best of Mayer, Stone, or Pelty, he might just pass them on this list when his career is over, based on career value. In three of four seasons from 2004 to 2007, Marquis posted an ERA+ of 101 or higher, and he had at least $191^2/_3$ innings pitched in all four years. His 2008 was also good, ERA+ of 100, though in just 167 innings.

He continued his role as innings eater for the 2008 Cubs,

who scored enough runs to make his starts pretty valuable. He should continue to inch up the Jewish victories leader board—at 79 through 2008, good for seventh place, he should, with another five seasons, push his way to third, trailing just Ken Holtzman and Sandy Koufax.

Certainly, more was expected of Marquis when he was selected in the first round of the 1996 draft by Atlanta, ahead of Jacque Jones, Milton Bradley, and Jimmy Rollins. He was a key part of the trade between Atlanta and St. Louis that brought J. D. Drew to the Braves.

But those ready to write him off after his terrible 2006 (14–16, 6.02 ERA) were also mistaken. Perhaps the Cubs overpaid him, giving him a three-year, $20 million deal. Since coming to Chicago, he's been the same Jason Marquis he was prior to 2006—a durable, middle-of-the-rotation starting pitcher. That certainly is worth around $6.5 million a year in today's salaries.

A bonus with Marquis: the 2005 Silver Slugger winner posted two of the top 11 single-season batting averages by starting pitchers from 2000 to 2007, with a .292 mark in 2004 and a .310 mark in 2005. His averages have slipped since, but his career .206/.227/.306 mark is excellent for any pitcher this side of Micah Owings.

## 5. Barry Latman

*Bats Right, Throws Right*
*Chicago White Sox, 1957–1959*
*Cleveland Indians, 1960–1963*

*Los Angeles Angels, 1964–1965*
*Houston Astros, 1966–1967*

While questions about the extent of Ty Cobb's racism continue to be debated, with compelling arguments on both sides, there is little evidence that Cobb was anti-Semitic. In fact, as unlikely as it may seem, given Cobb's background and reputation, it would not be a stretch to call Cobb a friend to the Jews.

Well, maybe not a friend. Cobb did, according to *Cobb*, Al Stump's biography, start an on-field brawl by telling A's player Claude Rossman that a member of the Tigers had called him "a Jew bastard." These apparently being fighting words, Rossman and the Tiger got into a fight, getting Rossman ejected. This isn't likely to win Ty Cobb any B'nai B'rith awards, but as anti-Semitism goes, it's pretty tame by 1909 standards.

But by the 1950s, Cobb had become a friend to young Barry Latman, who, unlike Rossman, actually was Jewish. Latman was a star at Fairfax High School in Los Angeles and teammates with fellow Jew and future major leaguer Larry Sherry. Latman's father, according to the April 2, 1958, issue of *The Sporting News*, got Latman an audience with Cobb.

"I was feeling pretty cocky," Latman told *The Sporting News*. "I had just pitched a perfect game [in high school] and was on top of the world. A friend of my father knew Mr. Cobb and took me to see him at Palo Alto. This was in 1953 and Mr. Cobb really brought me down to earth. I'll always be grateful for his interest."

According to Latman, five years after that conversation, the two still corresponded, including an eight-page letter from Cobb that spring. Will this get Cobb a statue in Sunrise, Florida? Probably not. But I'd think twice before putting his portrait on the sidewalk so that all the Jewish ladies can run over him with their walkers.

As for the recipient of Cobb's advice, Latman turned into a pretty solid major league pitcher. He was a swingman, a starter-reliever hybrid that has all but disappeared in the modern game, and unjustly so. Between 1959 and 1964, Latman started between 18 and 21 games, while relieving in 16 to 27 games each season, save one year when he relieved in 11 contests.

He performed in this role for the 1959 American League champion Chicago White Sox, posting an 8–5, 3.75 ERA season. In 1961 he went 13–5, 4.02 ERA for Cleveland, earning an All-Star Game berth in the process. Given how relievers were not held in high esteem at the time, this is fairly remarkable. But his first-half numbers—8–0, 2.90 ERA—could not be overlooked.

Two other notes about Latman: he was a professional singer before coming to baseball, singing with the Bob Mitchell Boys Choir, which appeared in numerous films and recorded with Bing Crosby and Frank Sinatra.

The other note is that Latman's rookie season, 1958 (he had pitched 12$\frac{1}{3}$ innings in 1957), was on par with the debut of Joba Chamberlain. Latman pitched 47$\frac{2}{3}$ innings in 1958, with a 0.76 ERA and just one home run allowed.

Chamberlain pitched to a 0.38 ERA, but in 24 innings. But Chamberlain's innings all came in relief. Latman started three games and punctuated his season with a complete-game shutout September 26, striking out nine batters in a 1–0 win. Chamberlain's rookie year was awfully impressive, but it is hard to say that Latman's wasn't more so.

### 6. Saul Rogovin

*Bats Right, Throws Right*
*Detroit Tigers, 1949–1951*
*Chicago White Sox, 1951–1953*
*Baltimore Orioles, 1955*
*Philadelphia Phillies, 1955–1957*

Living up to the idea that we are the "people of the book," Saul Rogovin went on to a successful career as a New York City high school English teacher. But the Brooklyn-born Rogovin prefaced his time teaching Hemingway with a solid, often spectacular baseball career, earning an ERA title while battling a persistent sore arm.

Rogovin was actually a third baseman for Lincoln High School in Brooklyn, and early in his minor league career as well. He was a pretty fair one, posting back-to-back seasons hitting over .280 for Chattanooga of the Southern Association. But on the last day of the 1945 season, he was asked to pitch and delivered a four-hit shutout. His hot corner days were over.

Rogovin eventually found himself with Buffalo of the International League, where he managed to lead a staff full of major leaguers. Rogovin won 13 games in 1948 and 16 in 1949, each year with an ERA under 4. Bob Hooper, Clem Houseman, and Luis Aloma, all of whom pitched in the major leagues as well, had higher ERAs than Rogovin.

The Detroit Tigers took notice and acquired Rogovin. But Detroit pitched him only sparingly. He had trouble cracking a deep rotation in 1950 that helped Detroit win 95 games. After a slow start in 1951, the Tigers dealt Rogovin to the Chicago White Sox for the forgettable Bob Cain.

The Tigers had reason to immediately regret the decision. Rogovin was fantastic for the White Sox, posting 192²/₃ innings of 2.48 ERA pitching. His overall season ERA of 2.78 was the best mark in the American League, and even when adjusted for park and era, Rogovin's mark ranked best in the circuit. He finished 12–8 for the Sox, but this is misleading: Rogovin lost seven decisions by one run and his eighth by a 2–0 score. A little luck, and Rogovin would have been 16–4; a lot of luck, and Rogovin could well have been 20–0.

Evidence of the good Rogovin/bad Rogovin split became clearer in 1952, and again, injuries were likely to blame. In a glowing March 5, 1952, profile in *The Sporting News*, Rogovin is noted as the "first to sign" with Chicago. That certainly indicates, following his tremendous 1951, that he had an interest in getting his contract in order, in case his arm didn't hold up.

But for much of 1952, his arm did hold up. He posted a career-high 14 wins, with a respectable 3.85 ERA. He finished in the top 10 in both strikeouts and shutouts—when he was on, he was terrific. Of course, take his three shutouts out of the equation, and his ERA in the other games was 4.35.

Rogovin slipped to 7–12, 5.22 ERA in 1953, and was sent to Cincinnati. But the Reds stowed him in the minor leagues, leaving him to pitch for a year in Havana. He put up pretty good numbers, 8–8, 3.65 ERA, which earned him a return to the major leagues in 1954 with Baltimore, and manager Paul Richards, who had him in Buffalo and Chicago. Rogovin struggled with the Orioles and landed with the Phillies, where he pitched, intermittently well, through 1957.

Rogovin's numbers are pretty fair to him. He finished 48–48, with a 4.06 ERA. They point to a pitcher who was, on the whole, average, and that is what Rogovin provided over his career. But it is certainly fair to assume that a healthy Rogovin would have provided far more than the average. One hopes Rogovin graded his students on a curve, and so will we.

### 7. Harry Feldman

*Bats Right, Throws Right*
*New York Giants, 1941–1946*

Harry Feldman grew up in the Bronx, threw for Clark Junior High School and Textile High, and signed with his hometown New York Giants. But in baseball, one usually goes through the minor leagues, and Feldman was no different.

After a 13–1 season with Class D Blytheville of the Northeast Arkansas League, Feldman spent two years with Class C Fort Smith of the Western Association. The second season, he posted a 25–9 mark. He also met his wife and converted to Christianity some time later.

If only Feldman's mother had a better understanding of baseball's farm systems, perhaps this could have been avoided. Sure, signing with the hometown team seemed like the best move. But even if Feldman had signed with Philadelphia, he might have played with the Trenton Senators, met a woman who knew how to make a seder . . .

But what chances did Feldman have of marrying within the faith, spending two years in Fort Smith, Arkansas? According to the Union of Reform Judaism, there is one synagogue in Fort Smith, with a total membership of 22. As of the 2000 census, the town population was 80,268. And the best-known athlete from Fort Smith is a running back named Priest.

Feldman finished with a 35–35 mark, along with a 3.80 ERA, good for an ERA+ of 96. But his combination of walks (91 in 1944, eighth highest in the league) and home runs (a top five finish in both 1944 and 1945) meant that when soldiers returned from World War II, there wasn't a major league place for Harry. Feldman added to that likelihood by jumping to the Mexican League. When it folded, baseball was reluctant to find places for the players that left.

Feldman returned to Fort Smith after retirement, opened a record store, but only made it to age 42. So much for country living.

## 8. Jason Hirsh

*Bats Right, Throws Right*
*Houston Astros, 2006*
*Colorado Rockies, 2007–*

Jason Hirsh has the talent to blow the other right-handed Jewish starters away. Hirsh stands 6'8", which is impressive in and of itself—the tallest Jewish player in history, and someone who could look Eddie Gaedel in the eye if he were standing on the shoulders of a second Eddie Gaedel.

But Hirsh's combination of strikeout ability and control is what makes him such an appealing prospect. Despite playing in hitter-friendly minor leagues for the lion's share of his apprenticeship time, Hirsh still posted a 3.44 ERA in 583 1/3 minor league innings, with 419 strikeouts and 161 walks. This success came despite a jump not from a Division I college power, but Division II California Lutheran, which took a chance on the mammoth high schooler, hoping for, and getting, a jump in velocity as he grew into his body.

Hirsh has been unlucky thus far on the injury front, breaking a leg to lose out on the chance to pitch in Colorado's improbable playoff march in 2007, and missing much of the 2008 season with rotator cuff soreness. But unlike pitchers in Saul Rogovin's time, injured hurlers get the chance to heal. And if Hirsh gets the chance to pitch extensively for the Rockies, building on his 2007 numbers (a 4.81 ERA is good for an ERA+ of 100 in Colorado), he'll be considerably higher on this list by the time he's through.

Let no one, however, doubt his toughness. He broke his

leg in the first inning of his final 2007 start, but he went on to pitch six innings, allowing just two earned runs. A quality start is tough enough to come by, let alone from a pitcher with a fracture.

### 9. Richard Conger
*Bats Right, Throws Right*
*Detroit Tigers, 1940*
*Pittsburgh Pirates, 1941–1942*
*Philadelphia Phillies, 1943*
Richard Conger was the UCLA bookend to the USC story of Jewish left fielder Al Silvera. Conger signed with the Tigers after just one year of college, and the Tigers threw him right into the major league fire. Conger actually did pretty well, allowing one run over three innings for the Tigers, who then sent him to Beaumont.

The Pirates grabbed him in the Rule V draft, and Conger put up ERAs of 3.34 in 1941 and 3.39 in 1942 for Pittsburgh's minor league affiliates in Albany and Toronto, but got just 12⅓ innings with the big league club. It's hard to figure: Conger allowed just 2 earned runs in those innings, good for an ERA over the two seasons of 1.46.

Once Conger posted an 11–6, 1.96 ERA for Toronto in 1943, the major leagues could ignore him no longer. Unfortunately, he bombed in his trial with the Phillies in 1943, putting up a 6.09 ERA over 24 games, including 18 starts.

Conger headed west to pitch for his hometown Los Angeles Angels of the Pacific Coast League and went 13–7,

2.88 ERA, with just 35 walks in 169 innings. That's the type of line that normally gets a player another big league shot, but instead Conger headed into military service for the tail end of World War II. Upon returning, he simply wasn't the same pitcher. He pitched until 1950, but never again with his prewar effectiveness.

### 10. Bob Katz
*Bats Right, Throws Right*
*Cincinnati Reds, 1944*
Bob Katz was another World War II major leaguer, a 13-year minor league veteran who got the call-up to the Reds the same season as 15-year-old Joe Nuxhall, the youngest player in major league history.

Nuxhall got the call after Katz failed—he was called up on June 10, while Katz played from May 12 to May 31. In six games, including two starts, Katz posted an ERA of 3.93, good for an ERA+ of 89. But his total work was just 18 1/3 innings—not indicative of particularly long starting assignments.

Katz went on to become an innings eater for AAA Toronto of the International League in 1945. In a year that had far more victories than defeats for America, Katz managed 20 wins of his own—but also 20 losses. His 4.05 ERA indicates that he was neither lucky nor unlucky, just a .500 pitcher with a whole lot of decisions. And, unlike his big league time, he pretty clearly went deep into games.

## 11. Mike Saipe

*Bats Right, Throws Right*
*Colorado Rockies, 1998*

Mike Saipe was so close to a storybook debut. Pitching at home for the Colorado Rockies on July 25, 1998, he'd allowed just three runs over six innings at the offensive cauldron that is Coors Field. With one out in the ninth, the Rockies led, 5–3.

"I know anything can happen in this game, but when there was one out in the ninth, I sort of smelled it that I could come out with a 'W,'" Saipe told the *Denver Post* that evening.

But then destiny met Dave Veres, who served up a game-tying home run to Derek Bell. It was as close as Saipe would come to a victory in the big leagues.

Saipe was crushed in his second start at Seattle, allowing home runs to Edgar Martinez and Ken Griffey Jr., and two to David Segui.

But let's not focus on the negatives. Here's Saipe, to the *Denver Post* back when he got the call-up, on June 25, 1998.

"I'm not going to be able to express the way I feel," he said. "I've never had this feeling before. It's obviously the high point in my life. This is reaching the top of my profession. This is what everybody's goal is. So, am I excited? Yeah, I'm really excited. But I haven't thought too deep about it because I'm living it."

No sympathy necessary for Saipe, who also, it should be

noted, won 67 games in the minor leagues. He briefly got to live out his dream. Dave Veres may have taken away his victory (and Veres, who blew 36 saves, was no stranger to the feeling), but Saipe knows he succeeded, for one night, on the highest level.

### 12. Leo Fishel
*Bats Right, Throws Right*
*New York Giants, 1899*
According to the excellent SABR biography by Jane Jacobs, Leo Fishel gave up his youthful dreams of major league success in order to pursue a career as a lawyer.

It is hard to argue with the idea that in a different financial time for baseball, Fishel might have chosen differently. According to the Jacobs bio, Fishel was once offered $20 to pitch a single semipro game for a White Plains, New York, team against (presumably) archrival Tarrytown; at the time, he was renting his law office for $7 a month.

He received a mixed review for his one professional starting effort, which took place on May 3, 1899. *The Sporting News* said the following of Fishel in the May 6 edition: "He has good curves, but was a bit unsteady in the second and fourth innings. Fishel gave the locals several chances to score by his wildness, but the team could not make hits when they were needed." Philadelphia beat the Giants, 7–3.

No such reviews would be possible for Fishel's law practice, which expanded, moved to Mineola, and allowed for Fishel to become town counsel for Hempstead.

Fishel didn't let his baseball connections drop, according to Jacobs. In 1905 he coached Freeport High School. His shortstop, George Morton Levy, went on to become his law partner. I think it is safe to assume there was a dominant entry in any Long Island legal softball leagues for quite some time.

### 13. Jeff Stember

*Bats Right, Throws Right*
*San Francisco Giants, 1980*

Eighty-one years after one Jewish pitcher, Leo Fishel, made his major league debut for the Giants, another did so, this time for the San Francisco version of the franchise in the Astrodome.

Stember struggled through the first three innings, walking a pair, but had allowed only one earned run, thanks to a first-inning home run by Terry Puhl. The Giants trailed 3–1, however, as a Rennie Stennett error in the third had led to two more Houston runs.

With manager Dave Bristol managing for his job, he pinch-hit for Stember, hoping Max Venable could come through with the bases loaded. Venable did, and the Giants went on to win the game, but Stember did not get the victory.

Would Stember have been allowed to hit in a 1–1 game in the fourth? As the pitcher who replaced Stember in the game, Joaquin Andujar, once said, "There is one word in America that says it all, and that one word is, 'You never know.'"

| NAME | GAMES | INNINGS | ERA+ | W-L | Additional |
|------|-------|---------|------|-----|------------|
| 1. Barney Pelty | 266 | 1908 | 100 | 92–117 | |
| 2. Erskine Mayer | 245 | 1427 | 99 | 91–70 | 21 wins in 1914, 1915 |
| 3. Steve Stone | 320 | 1788.3 | 98 | 107–93 | 1980 Cy Young |
| 4. Jason Marquis | 257 | 1269 | 97 | 79–70 | 15 wins in 2004 |
| 5. Barry Latman | 344 | 1219 | 94 | 59–68 | 1961 All-Star |
| 6. Saul Rogovin | 150 | 883.7 | 96 | 48–48 | 2.51 ERA in 1951 |
| 7. Harry Feldman | 143 | 666 | 96 | 35–35 | |
| 8. Jason Hirsh | 32 | 165.7 | 88 | 8–11 | |
| 9. Richard Conger | 19 | 70 | 67 | 3–7 | |
| 10. Bob Katz | 6 | 18.3 | 89 | 0–1 | |
| 11. Mike Saipe | 2 | 10 | 48 | 0–1 | |
| 12. Leo Fishel | 1 | 9 | 62 | 0–1 | |
| 13. Jeff Stember | 1 | 3 | 118 | 0–0 | |

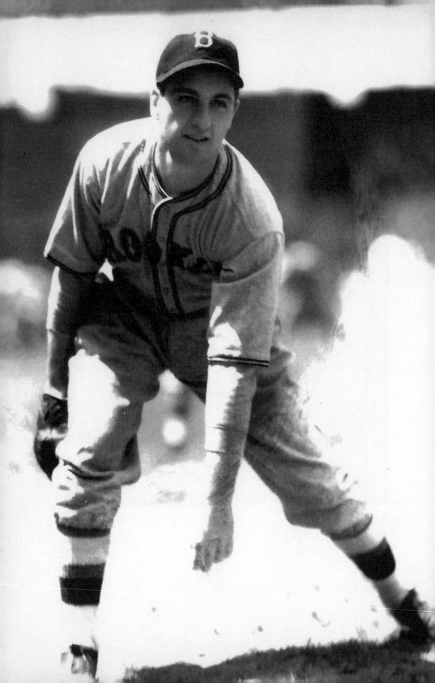

# Left-Handed Relievers

There are a number of quality left-handed relievers among Jewish players. However, two in particular stand out among them.

Scott Radinsky and Harry Eisenstat were used very differently by the teams that employed them. Radinsky was frequently a short reliever, saving as many as 15 games in a season. Eisenstat was a starter for 20 percent of his major league games. Radinsky's innings high was 71$^1$/$_3$. Eisenstat passed that mark three times, twice pitching more than 125 innings in a season.

But both pitchers were extremely effective. Radinsky's ERA+ over his 481$^2$/$_3$ was 118; Eisenstat's ERA+ over 478$^2$/$_3$ innings was 114. Give Eisenstat the edge for three reasons.

*Harry Eisenstat*

First, 20 percent of Eisenstat's games, and well over 20 percent of his innings, came as a starting pitcher; his ERA is certainly higher than it would be had he simply been relieving.

Second, Eisenstat was traded, straight up, for Earl Averill, a Hall of Famer. While Radinsky was quite valuable, no one was ever trading a Hall of Famer for Scott Radinsky.

Third, at the end of his career, Scott Radinsky went on to sing lead for Pulley, a punk band. At the end of his career, Harry Eisenstat fought in World War II, rising to the level of second lieutenant to help defeat the Nazis. Now, this may be my anti–punk music bias showing, but I am hard-pressed to think of a single punk album that rises to the level of defeating the Nazis.

### 1. Harry Eisenstat

*Bats Left, Throws Left*
*Brooklyn Dodgers, 1935–1937*
*Detroit Tigers, 1938–1939*
*Cleveland Indians, 1939–1942*

On the final day of the 1938 season, with America's Jews, and baseball fans in general, riveted by Hank Greenberg's pursuit of Babe Ruth's single-season home run record, Harry Eisenstat almost made history of his own pitching for the Tigers.

Greenberg stood at 58 home runs, two short of the Babe's 60, entering the final day of the season, which called for a game against the Cleveland Indians. Greenberg was facing

Bob Feller, who was kryptonite to his home run hitting. And Feller was on, striking out 18 Tigers on the afternoon.

Harry Eisenstat was better. Eisenstat took a no-hitter into the eighth inning and beat the great Feller, 4–1. It was not the type of game conducive to a home run chase—Greenberg finished with 58. But had Eisenstat turned the trick, he'd have produced the first no-hitter in Jewish baseball history. Instead it was—who else?—Sandy Koufax who notched Judaism's first no-no on June 30, 1962—though if we're being literal, Judaism's first no-no was probably "Do not have any other gods before Me."

While Eisenstat and Radinsky were close, based on career value, it is clear that Eisenstat lost most likely more than half of his total career to World War II. He had a fantastic season for Cleveland in 1942, posting a 2.45 ERA over 47 innings for an ERA+ of 140, before entering military service.

By 1945, according to the *Utah Historic Quarterly*, he was still in the service, playing for a Provo, Utah, semipro team between deployments and displaying such control that his catcher, Don Overly, said even "his bad pitches are so close to being good that they could be called the other way."

So clearly, the control that allowed him to post a paltry walk rate of 2.1 per nine innings had not deserted him.

## 2. Scott Radinsky
*Chicago White Sox, 1990–1993, 1995*
*Los Angeles Dodgers, 1996–1998*

*St. Louis Cardinals, 1999–2000*
*Cleveland Indians, 2001*

Though Scott Radinsky didn't help to defeat the Nazis (and in fairness to Radinsky, by the time he was born, 1968, the only Nazis left were in hiding in South America), his valor under the duress of severe medical problems should not be minimized.

Radinsky was highly regarded coming out of high school, selected as a third-round pick in the 1986 draft by the Chicago White Sox, 30 slots ahead of Bo Jackson. Radinsky eventually excelled in the minors after his first two years were marked by control issues. His 1989 in A-ball, 1.75 ERA, 83 strikeouts in 61$^{2}$/$_{3}$ innings for South Bend of the Midwest League, earned him a shot at making the 1990 White Sox out of spring training, and he did just that.

Radinsky had a solid rookie year, though his first half was far better than his second half—his ERA jumped from 2.12 prior to the break to 9.82 afterward. But in 1991, Radinsky was effective all season long, putting up a 2.02 ERA in 71$^{1}$/$_{3}$ innings, good for an ERA+ of 197. He followed with a similarly effective 1993—2.73 ERA in 59$^{2}$/$_{3}$ innings—but his performance dropped off in 1993.

While it can't be known what role it played, a likely reason for Radinsky's reduced effectiveness could well have been that he had Hodgkin's disease, which cost Radinsky the 1994 season. He returned in 1995 but posted a 5.45 ERA and struck out just 14 in 38 innings, well off his career norms.

He took a pay cut of nearly 50 percent and returned to his hometown Los Angeles Dodgers in 1996, and there, his early-career effectiveness returned. Radinsky posted three fantastic relief seasons in a row, pitching in an average of 65 games per season, with ERAs of 2.41, 2.89, and 2.63. Even in pitcher-friendly Dodger Stadium, that was good for ERA+ marks of 161, 134, and 153. Three seasons of elite relief pitching would be impressive enough; to do so as a cancer survivor only multiplies the impact of his performance.

Radinsky finished his career with the Cardinals and Indians, and even battled back from Tommy John surgery to play a final season with Calgary of the Pacific Coast League.

And while he has continued in baseball, now the pitching coach for the Buffalo Bisons, in the Cleveland Indians organization, his musical career is threatening to eclipse his pitching one, having recorded nine albums with his punk band Pulley.

Relief pitchers, lefties especially, have a reputation for being complicated. But this isn't Sparky-Lyle-sits-naked-on-a-birthday-cake complicated. Radinsky is, by any standards, a renaissance man.

### 3. Scott Schoeneweis

*Anaheim Angels, 1999–2003*
*Chicago White Sox, 2003–2004*
*Toronto Blue Jays, 2005–2006*
*Cincinnati Reds, 2006*
*New York Mets, 2007–*

Coincidentally, Scott Schoeneweis, like Scott Radinsky, is a left-handed relief pitcher who has survived both cancer and Tommy John surgery to become an outstanding major leaguer. In essence, the difference between Radinsky and Schoeneweis is that while both were devastating against lefties, Radinsky handled righties nearly as well, while Schoeneweis struggles mightily against them.

Schoeneweis grew up in South Jersey. Going on to Duke, he had a sensational freshman year, followed by a diagnosis of testicular cancer that spread to his lymph nodes. Through aggressive chemotherapy—he told the *New York Post* on October 18, 2002, that he "took six months of chemotherapy in three months"—he was able to return to the baseball team the following year, when he promptly blew out his elbow, requiring Tommy John surgery.

Either of these problems could have ended another person's career—and the cancer could have done much worse than that. But Schoeneweis instead returned to form his senior year, graduated with a degree in history, and was drafted in the third round of the 1996 draft by the Angels, four picks ahead of Nationals first baseman Nick Johnson.

It isn't quite clear why it took the Angels so long to make Schoeneweis into a reliever; he didn't have a tremendous amount of success as a starter in the minors. He went 7–10, 5.45 ERA in 2000 as a starter for the Angels, who promptly tabbed him as opening day starter in 2001. He went 10–11 with a 5.08 ERA in 2001, and 6–6 with a 5.38 ERA as a starter in 2002 before being moved to the bullpen, where he pitched to a 3.25 ERA as the Angels won a World Series.

Schoeneweis's Achilles' heel is right-handed batters. His line against lefties stands at .224/.299/.295, while against righties, he is at .294/.367/.469. Years after teams had discovered this, his 2007 manager, Willie Randolph, used him repeatedly against righties, subjecting him to unjust booing from the Shea Stadium crowd, even as he put up his customary .204/.308/.247 line against left-handed batters.

Schoeneweis has a terrific sense of humor and is one of the more enjoyable interviews in the New York Mets clubhouse. He claims he didn't hear cheers, but the absence of boos at the start of what was a far more effective year for the Mets was "kind of eerie. You get used to it, I guess. It's like people who live in the city and move to the country, how they can't sleep nights."

As usual, there is truth behind every joke. And for Schoeneweis, who is as effective as a lefty specialist as he's ever been, the truth is he's been through, and weathered admirably, far worse than an angry Shea crowd.

### 4. John Grabow
*Pittsburgh Pirates, 2003–*
If Terry Bradshaw is the favorite son of Pittsburgh, then John Grabow certainly holds the title for the Pittsburgh suburb of Squirrel Hill, which is host to 16 Jewish congregations and nearly half-Jewish, according to a September 12, 2007, article in the *Pittsburgh Tribune-Review*.

Grabow told Jonathan Mayo of JewishSports.com in 2004 that he welcomes the attention of the Jewish community, and even his appearance in the Jewish Major Leaguers baseball card set. "That would be something that would be cool," Grabow said. "My grandmother would really like that. And she'll get a kick out of the card."

Grabow has been a fixture in the Pirates bullpen for six seasons and over that time has a career ERA+ of 103. But he is more valuable than that would suggest. For one thing, he is reasonably effective against both lefties and righties. For another, though he has a fine strikeout and walk rate, he does pitch to contact a good bit in front of what have been poor defensive teams year after year. Errors alone do not account for the lack of range exhibited by many Pirates fielders during Grabow's tenure. On a better team, Grabow's ERA+ would certainly have been better. Each of the past three seasons, Baseball Prospectus has Grabow's DERA—which subtracts defense from ERA computation—as a half-run lower than his actual number.

Grabow was drafted in the third round of the 1997 draft, ahead of Eric Byrnes, Chone Figgins, and Xavier Nady. But Grabow, who didn't turn 30 until November 4, 2008, is still coming into his own. With a career strikeout rate of nearly 9 per nine innings and a walk rate that has been slashed over his past few seasons, Grabow, if healthy, should be able to maintain his effectiveness well into his 30s. By the time he's finished, he has a decent chance of pushing to the top of this list.

## 5. Craig Breslow
*Bats Left, Throws Left*
*San Diego Padres, 2005*
*Boston Red Sox, 2006*
*Cleveland Indians, 2008*
*Minnesota Twins, 2008*

Craig Breslow took the clichéd double-major-in-molecular-physics-and-biochemistry-at-Yale path to the major leagues. (In my companion book, *The Molecular Physician Baseball Talmud*, Breslow ranks at the top of virtually every list.) He was the first Eli to make the major leagues since Ron Darling.

As you can tell from his majors, Breslow was going to live the Jewish mother's dream and become a doctor. But as he told Baseball Prospectus in a December 18, 2006, interview, "That was the contingency plan if baseball didn't work out, but it kind of gets tucked further away as I have more success. I guess it still is, but hopefully I'll have 15 years in the game and I won't have to think about it for awhile. That said, I've always felt strongly about medicine and it's something I'll keep as an option. We'll see when the time comes."

That time certainly hasn't come yet. Breslow had a dominant year in 2008, with 47 innings of 1.91 ERA, good for an ERA+ of 221. Control had been a problem, but Breslow walked just 19 in 47 innings, striking out 39.

If anyone can figure out how to alter mechanics to throw more pitches in the strike zone, it likely is Breslow. Having turned 28 in August 2008, he still has time to adjust. And given his success against both lefties and righties, Breslow can be a valuable pitcher for years to come.

## 6. Steve Rosenberg

*Chicago White Sox, 1988–1990*
*San Diego Padres, 1991*

The Rosenbergs had a tough century plus here in America. Julius and Ethel Rosenberg were executed for treason. Ken Rosenberg, a character in several versions of Grand Theft Auto, has an addiction to cocaine. And Richie Rosenberg, a member of the Max Weinberg 7 informally known as La Bamba, is a frequent butt of Conan O'Brien's jokes.

The Rosenbergs have had very little major league success, too, though three Rosenbergs have played major league baseball. Steve Rosenberg is the most accomplished of the three, and he posted a WARP3 value of just 1.5 for his career, according to Baseball Prospectus. His career ERA+ was just 78, and his season high was a mere 92.

He was traded to the Mets in the winter of 1991, but he never got the chance to play for his hometown team. This might be considered a minor tragedy by some, but relatively speaking, he got off easy. If you don't believe me, ask Ethel.

## 7. Marv Rotblatt

*Bats Both, Throws Left*
*Chicago White Sox, 1948, 1950–1951*

In today's era, Marv Rotblatt probably never would have gotten the chance to pitch at the major league level, due simply to his height. Baseball-Reference.com lists him at 5'7"; an April 25, 1951, profile of Rotblatt in *The Sporting News* lists him at 5'8".

The diminutive Rotblatt was remarkable for his time, but there were other exceptions to the tall pitcher rule, such as Bobby Shantz, who stood just 5'4". But in the 2008 season, just one pitcher, Tom Gordon, is listed at even 5'9". Seven more check in at 5'10", and another 24 stand at 5'11". Every other major league pitcher is 6' or taller.

But Rotblatt's changeup, called "the best I've ever seen" by then manager Paul Richards, was his ticket to the big leagues. Rotblatt was, like Saul Bellow's Augie March, Chicago-born; he then earned a degree in journalism at the University of Illinois. He had brief stops in the majors in both 1948 and 1950, throwing a combined 27 innings. He seemed to put the minors in his rearview mirror in 1950, when he posted a 22–9, 2.67 ERA with Memphis of the AA Southern Association.

"Best advice about pitching success I ever heard came from Hugh Mulcahy while I was at Memphis," Rotblatt said in that same *Sporting News* profile. "Be able to get your breaking stuff over the plate when you're behind and you'll be a winning pitcher."

The problem with Mulcahy providing advice on being a "winning pitcher," of course, is that his nickname was Hugh "Losing Pitcher" Mulcahy, and his career record was 45–89. Rotblatt posted a 3.40 ERA in 47 2/3 innings, good for an ERA+ of 119, but never reached the majors again, posting mediocre minor league seasons in outposts like Memphis, Atlanta, Allentown, and Topeka.

The lesson: when receiving advice, consider the source.

## 8. Syd Cohen
*Bats Both, Throws Left*
*Washington Senators, 1934, 1936–1937*

Syd Cohen was a man of changing identities. He began his professional career as an outfielder, but he became a pitcher. He started his collegiate career as a member of the Crimson Tide, but he became a Southern Methodist Mustang. Playing in the United States, he was Syd Cohen; when he played in Mexico, he changed his name to Pablo Garcia.

Cohen pitched parts of three seasons in the major leagues, posting ERA+ marks of 58, 91, and 143. But despite the improvement, and a career ERA+ mark of 100 in 109 innings, he never saw major league action after the age of 31. He did pitch in the minors until age 49, even returning to Mexico 19 years after he appeared as an outfielder, and once again, under the name Pablo Garcia.

Thanks to Syd and his brother Andy, Cohens easily outpace Rosenbergs in total WARP3 value. This is not surprising: Cohen is the 270th most popular surname in the United States, according to PBS.org, while Rosenberg ranks 1,489th. Of course, both WARP3 totals rank well behind Greenberg, though it is only the 1,237th most popular name in the United States—but that is largely due to one particular Greenberg.

## 9. Tony Cogan

*Bats Left, Throws Left*
*Kansas City Royals, 2001*

It's getting late in the career for Tony Cogan, who pitched at age 32 for the Independent League Gary SouthShore Rail-Cats in 2008. He's been effective in the league, which has sent a number of players to the major leagues. He posted a 2.77 ERA and 25 saves in 2007 as Gary's closer, and pitched effectively in 2008 as a starter for the RailCats.

But generally, 32 is old for a prospect to get a second look, though fellow Northern League alum Chris Coste did just write a book entitled *The 33-Year-Old Rookie*. Cogan did not impress in his 24²/₃ big league innings with Kansas City, posting a 5.84 ERA, with 13 walks and 17 strikeouts. His ERA+ was 83, and even for a pitching-starved team like the Royals, that wasn't enough to get it done.

But even if he doesn't return to the major leagues, Cogan can provide a role model for Gary, Indiana's Jewish population. According to Sperling's Best Places, 0.41 percent of Gary's 97,715 people are Jewish—an estimated total Jewish population in the city of an even 400.

In other words: if not Tony Cogan, then who?

## 10. Andrew Lorraine

*Bats Left, Throws Left*
*California Angels, 1994*
*Chicago White Sox, 1995*
*Oakland Athletics, 1997*

*Seattle Mariners, 1998*
*Chicago Cubs, 1999–2000*
*Cleveland Indians, 2000*
*Milwaukee Brewers, 2001*

Andrew Lorraine, like Tony Cogan, is a product of Stanford University who has struggled to find regular major league work. Lorraine is still pitching, appearing for Cardenales de Lara of the Venezuelan Winter League in 2007. But he pitched to a 7.36 ERA in 11 innings—he may be at the end of the line.

Still, Lorraine made his mark along the way, pitching a complete-game shutout for the Cubs on August 6, 1999, the first Jewish pitcher to do so since Steve Stone on June 21, 1980.

As for his distinctive name, it was Levin, according to a September 22, 1999, article in the *Jewish World Review*. But his paternal grandfather, serving in the Alsace-Lorraine section of France during World War II, liked Lorraine so much he changed his surname.

Unfortunately for Lorraine, his last name sounds much prettier than his career ERA of 6.53 in 175 innings. Lorraine did find a large measure of success in the minor leagues, however—his career line is 104–80, with a 4.21 ERA, and with most of those innings coming in the hitter-friendly Pacific Coast League, that is even more impressive than it sounds.

### 11. Ed Mayer
*Bats Left, Throws Left*
*Chicago Cubs, 1958–1959*

It took Ed Mayer five years to reach the big leagues—and shortly after he did, his arm gave out. But as evidenced by the excellent biography of Mayer by Jim Sargent of the SABR Biography Project, he's far from bitter about this.

Mayer, a Cal Berkeley product who grew up in San Francisco, chased his major league dream from 1952 to 1957 in San Jose, California; Yuma, Arizona; Greensboro, North Carolina; Montgomery, Alabama; Omaha, Nebraska; Rochester, New York; and Fort Worth, Texas.

Maybe it was meeting Babe Ruth when he was 15 that did it; Ruth presented then-15-year-old Mayer with the MVP trophy for Mayer's American Legion All-Star Game.

After a mediocre start and two solid relief appearances in 1957, the Cubs converted Mayer into a full-time reliever in 1958. On April 17, 1958, he converted his only save opportunity, pitching $1\,^2/_3$ scoreless innings to help Chicago edge St. Louis, 9–8. But by June, in three of his final six appearances, he failed to retire a batter, and the Cubs sent him down.

"I pitched to the June cut-down date," Mayer told Sargent. "By then my arm was starting to be not so good. The Cubs noticed it. Fortunately, they sent me to Portland, and that was the end of my big league career."

Mayer claimed that he took a test in college that concluded he didn't want to be anything professionally, but he managed just fine after his baseball career ended. Not only did he teach in middle school for 25 years, but his crossword puzzles have appeared in *Games* magazine.

Still, the brief, shining major league moments for Mayer are captured on his vanity license plate: "OLD CUB."

## 12. Matt Ford
*Bats Both, Throws Left*
*Milwaukee Brewers, 2003*

Matt Ford was a victim of his own success. After a standout career in Coral Springs High School (Ford reversed the typical Jewish story and started his life in Broward County, rather than completing it there), he was a third-round pick in the 1999 draft by the Blue Jays, two picks ahead of Hank Blalock, two picks after Josh Bard.

Ford was slowly making his way up the Toronto organization's ladder, winning an ERA title for Dunedin of the high-A Florida State League, with a 2.37 ERA in 118 innings. That attracted the attention of the Milwaukee Brewers, who drafted Ford in the Rule V draft.

So Ford, rather than continuing his development, found himself making the jump from A-ball to the major leagues.

Ford pitched pretty well, particularly considering the circumstances of his debut. In $3^2/_3$ innings, Ford put up a 4.33 ERA, good for an ERA+ of 99, just below average. For context, Johan Santana, who made a similar jump after becoming a Rule V selection by Minnesota, pitched 86 innings with a 6.49 ERA, good for an ERA+ of 80.

But Ford has not been able to find his way back to the major leagues. Despite a solid 3.94 ERA with AA Huntsville of the Southern League in 2004, the Brewers released Ford.

He pitched to a 2.61 ERA with AAA Omaha after signing with the Royals, but Kansas City let him go. After his numbers dipped to a 4.50 ERA in 2006 with AAA Rochester of Minnesota's system, Ford couldn't get a position in affiliated baseball, and he has been trying to get noticed in the underrated independent Atlantic League.

In 2008 he played in Bridgeport, Connecticut, pitching with the Bluefish and trying to catch on with some team that needs a lefty in the bullpen. Just 28 as of April 2009, he has time on his side—but lately, not results.

### 13. Bob Tufts

*Bats Left, Throws Left*
*San Francisco Giants, 1981*
*Kansas City Royals, 1982–1983*

Like Craig Breslow, Tufts is another Jewish player with an Ivy League pedigree, with an undergraduate degree from Princeton and an MBA from Columbia. Here is what the Jewish Ivy League team would look like:

> C Moe Berg (Princeton)
> P Craig Breslow (Yale)
> P Bob Tufts (Princeton)
> P Leo Fishel (Columbia)
> P Bob Davis (Yale)

So you'd need a lot of strikeouts. But you'd have the pitching depth to do it.

Tufts is a member of a number of select groups. He is also one of the Jewish players who converted to Judaism, finding inspiration in his study of the Holocaust while at Princeton.

Tufts's ERA also fails to do him justice. While he posted an ERA of 4.71 in 42 major league frames, good for an ERA+ of just 81, he struck out 28 in those 42 innings and walked just 14. It was his batting average against of .328 that kept him from major league success.

Strangely enough, his batting average against when facing righties was .328, and his BAA when facing lefties was . . . 328. That doesn't seem coincidental; that must be the work of a witch!

And it was. Tufts told Murray Chass of the *New York Times* on September 21, 2005, that "I have a relative (Elizabeth Morse) who was the first woman tried and convicted of witchcraft in Essex County (Newbury, Mass., in 1680)." While Morse was subsequently pardoned, according to Tufts, we all know about the revolving door prison system in Massachusetts—it doesn't prove a thing.

Fortunately, Tufts has embraced Judaism more than witchcraft (as far as we know), even traveling to Israel in 2006 to teach the game of baseball, along with fellow Jewish convert Elliott Maddox, according to the April 19, 2007, edition of the *New Jersey Jewish News*.

Let's just hope nobody got the wrong idea when they saw him floating in the Dead Sea.

## 14. Roger Samuels

*Bats Left, Throws Left*
*San Francisco Giants, 1988*
*Pittsburgh Pirates, 1989*

If Roger Samuels had come along 20 years later, he'd have been a favorite of statheads everywhere. His strikeout rate, combined with his lack of major league chances, would have made him a cause célèbre. There'd be Free Roger Samuels Web sites, he'd be mentioned by any stat-savvy fan of a team that needed bullpen help, and his failure to find major league work would be roundly cited as proof that major league teams had no concept of how to put together a bullpen.

In 692 minor league innings, Samuels struck out 536, good for a relatively good strikeout rate of 6.97 per nine. But through age 26, that was even higher, at 7.08 per nine innings. He got a trial with the Giants in 1988 and struck out 22 in 23 1/3 innings, walking just 7. His ERA was a respectable 3.47, good for an ERA+ of 95, and the Pirates saw enough to deal veteran infielder Ken Oberkfell for Samuels.

But Samuels got just five games and 3 2/3 innings to prove himself in Pittsburgh, and he pitched to a 9.82 ERA for the Pirates. He returned to the minor leagues, where he posted good strikeout rates, and even reduced his walk rate considerably, which had been the one factor holding him back. But Samuels put up a 2.83 ERA for AAA Tidewater in the Mets system in 1990, then left the game. Apparently, there was no room for a strikeout pitcher with improving control who stood 6' 5".

If only he'd come along even a bit later, he might have revived his prospects in the independent league scene that emerged in the mid-1990s. He'd get inspirational e-mails from numbers crunchers, and some team might have taken another shot on him. Instead, Samuels fell short of what might well have been a solid major league career. By all indications, far lesser relievers have spent far more time in the major leagues.

### 15. Moe Savransky

*Bats Left, Throws Left*
*Cincinnati Reds, 1954*

Moe Savransky could have been a classmate of Ronald Patimkin, the older brother of Brenda in Philip Roth's *Goodbye, Columbus*. Savransky played baseball at Ohio State from 1948 to 1953. Considering that Brenda was an undergraduate in the story, Ronald was her older brother, and the book was released in 1959, Roth was writing it in the period of 1956–1958. That places Ronald right in the middle of Savransky's time there. Of course, the fact that Patimkin is fictional makes it unlikely that their paths crossed.

But it gives you an idea of what it meant for Savransky to be the star of Ohio State's baseball team, leading the Buckeyes to the College World Series in 1951. I like to think somewhere there is a record with Bill Stern's voiceover extolling the virtues of Moe Savransky.

But while Roth himself missed the Korean War, serving in 1955–1956, Moe Savransky's development time was interrupted by the Forgotten War in 1952–1953. There is no question he came back from the service as a different pitcher. In 1951, for Buffalo of the International League, Savransky pitched 195 innings with a 2.92 ERA. To put that in perspective, Tom Acker, who went on to pitch four league-average seasons in the big leagues, was at 3.69.

When Savransky returned, he spent 1954 with Cincinnati, posting a 4.88 ERA in 24 big league innings. The Reds sent him to AAA Charleston in 1955—he put up a 5.44 ERA in 134 innings. Picked up by Seattle of the Pacific Coast League near the end of 1955, he was even worse—6.14 ERA in 14²/₃ innings, even with a Jewish battery mate in Joe Ginsberg.

I hope Moe Savransky's father had a profitable bathroom appliance store, so that Moe had a fallback career. But unlike Ronald, who is portrayed as merely a good college athlete, Savransky, without the military interruption, was on track to be far more than that.

### 16. Mike Milchin
*Bats Left, Throws Left*
*Minnesota Twins, 1996*
*Baltimore Orioles, 1996*
Mike Milchin, a hard-throwing lefty, was selected in the second round of the 1989 draft by the St. Louis Cardinals, 33 picks ahead of Tim Salmon, 43 ahead of John Olerud, and 74 picks ahead of Jeff Bagwell. And had Milchin stayed healthy, the preceding sentence might not have seemed so crazy.

Milchin helped the U.S. Olympic Team to a gold medal in 1988, with a 4–1 record, 2 saves, and a 1.93 ERA. His strikeout rate at Clemson rose to 11.54 his senior year, and in his rookie season with Hamilton of the New York–Penn League, it stood at 10.02.

But it came steadily down as he faced more and more injuries. He broke a toe, his shoulder gave him problems, his knee required surgery—his career was like asking your great-uncle Sidney, "So, what's new?"

By the time he got to the major leagues, his ability to strike out hitters was still there—29 in 32 innings—but his command disappeared, as he allowed 6 home runs, 28 hits, and 17 walks in those innings with Minnesota and Baltimore.

Milchin is now an agent with SFX, an agency that represents some of the premier talents in baseball, such as David Ortiz, Pedro Martinez, and Jim Thome. With some luck on the injury front, Milchin could have been on that list, too.

### 17. Happy Foreman
*Bats Left, Throws Left*
*Chicago White Sox, 1924*
*Boston Red Sox, 1926*

A strong argument can be made that players in the old days enjoyed playing more than they do today. I cite not increasing salaries, or simple nostalgia, but the undeniable fact: 16 players had Happy as a part or all of their nicknames in major league history, and not one of them played after 1952.

Among the Happys, Foreman ranks around the middle

of the pack, far behind Happy Jack Chesbro, who made the Hall of Fame, and standouts like Happy Felsch, Happy Al Milnar, Happy Archer McKain, Happy Townsend, and, of course, the Happy Rabbit, Stan Rojek, known informally as the Last of the Happys.

But Foreman's $11\frac{1}{3}$ major league innings at an ERA+ of 128 puts him ahead of Happys ranging from Happy Pat Hartnett to Happy Iott, who was also known as Biddo.

Strangely, while Happys have fallen off, there has not been a corresponding rise in Grumpys—zero in major league history, at least officially. (Hard to understand how Barry Bonds avoided that tag.) The age of the Sleepys came much earlier—of the four Sleepys, Sleepy Bill Burns was the most modern, and he last played in 1912.

Bashfuls and Sneezys have never made the major leagues either, which is predictable—Bashful would probably take too many pitches, while Sneezy is asking for trouble, picking a profession primarily played on grass (and during spring and fall allergy season!). And the absence of Dopeys, in such a cerebral game, is certainly for the best.

And, as should surprise no one who saw the leadership role he provided to the Seven Dwarfs, there have been 85 Docs, stretched across seemingly every era of major league baseball. Roy Halladay has the nickname Doc today, while All-Stars ranging from Dwight Gooden to Doc Cramer have the honorary medical title.

Still, this reinforces my original point: who's happy when they spend time with the doctor?

## 18. Bud Swartz

*Bats Left, Throws Left*
*St. Louis Browns, 1947*

It is hard to view Bud Swartz's major league career, in which he allowed 4 earned runs and 7 walks in 5$^1$/$_3$ innings, as a success. In fairness to Swartz, he was just 18 when he got his only big league shot. Still, subsequent minor league success was limited, though he did win 11 games for Aberdeen, South Dakota, of the Class C Northern League, his ERA was 4.12, and he walked 69 in 131 innings.

However, Swartz is one of only 351 major leaguers to post a career batting average of 1.000, with one hit in one at bat. The undefeated batting record didn't carry over into his minor league career, where he hit just .164. But I choose to believe that Swartz was merely bored by lesser pitching, and the Browns missed a real opportunity to use Swartz any time the team needed a hit. Considering the team was in the midst of eight straight losing seasons, before the franchise moved to Baltimore, such a player would have come in handy.

## 19. Herb Karpel

*Bats Left, Throws Left*
*New York Yankees, 1946*

In the midst of an impressive minor league career that saw Herb Karpel win 128 games as a starting pitcher, seven times reaching double figures in victories and three times posting full-season ERAs at 2.53 or below, Karpel was summoned to New York to pitch in April 1946.

His appearances, sad to say, did not go well. In two games, April 19 and 20, he faced eight batters, and four got hits. Karpel's ERA was 10.80. He returned to Newark and posted a 14–8 record, 2.41 ERA. It wasn't enough to bring him back.

This is not a reflection on Karpel nearly as much as it is on the extremely small margin for error any pitcher had in a time of no guaranteed contracts, permanent ownership by one team due to the reserve clause, and 16 small pitching staffs. In today's game, Karpel, after six seasons in the minor leagues, would become a free agent and likely would draw interest from teams short a starting pitcher, which is basically everybody. But instead, Karpel resumed his stellar minor league career, and the major leagues never heard from him again.

## 20. Brian Bark

*Bats Left, Throws Left*
*Boston Red Sox, 1995*

On the heels of a solid 1995 season for AAA Pawtucket, Brian Bark received the reward many organizational soldiers receive, with a call-up to Boston for September. He pitched three games with the Red Sox, allowing two hits and a walk, no strikeouts, but also no runs.

His last pitch in the major leagues came September 8, 1995, against the Yankees, with two men on and Don Mattingly at the plate. Bark induced an inning-ending double play to get out of the inning. Not a bad way to go out.

## 21. Ed Wineapple

*Bats Left, Throws Left*
*Washington Senators, 1929*

While the Washington Senators fell to the Detroit Tigers, 16–2, on September 15, 1929, no one can claim that Ed Wineapple was the primary culprit among the Senators pitchers. Wineapple gave up just a pair of earned runs over four innings, walking three and striking out one.

It was his one moment of major league glory, though his minor league record indicates that he may have missed his true calling as a hitter—he was a .287 hitter in 164 minor league at bats, and 13 of his 47 hits went for extra bases, including 4 home runs.

During his one major league game, his innings doubtlessly helped the team. But Washington could have used some of those extra base hits, too.

| NAME | GAMES | INNINGS | ERA+ | SAVES | W-L | Additional |
|---|---|---|---|---|---|---|
| 1. Harry Eisenstat | 165 | 478.7 | 114 | 14 | 25–27 | Great swingman |
| 2. Scott Radinsky | 557 | 481.7 | 118 | 52 | 42–25 | |
| 3. Scott Schoeneweis | 517 | 934.3 | 94 | 9 | 45–55 | Lefty specialist |
| 4. John Grabow | 345 | 316 | 103 | 6 | 17–15 | |
| 5. Craig Breslow | 63 | 66.3 | 163 | 1 | 0–4 | |
| 6. Steve Rosenberg | 87 | 209.3 | 78 | 1 | 6–15 | |
| 7. Marv Rotblatt | 35 | 74.7 | 86 | 2 | 4–3 | |
| 8. Syd Cohen | 55 | 109 | 100 | 5 | 3–7 | |
| 9. Tony Cogan | 39 | 24.7 | 83 | 0 | 0–4 | |
| 10. Andrew Lorraine | 59 | 175 | 69 | 0 | 6–11 | |

| NAME | GAMES | INNINGS | ERA+ | SAVES | W-L | Additional |
|------|-------|---------|------|-------|-----|------------|
| 11. Ed Mayer | 22 | 31.3 | 91 | 1 | 2–2 | |
| 12. Matt Ford | 25 | 43.7 | 99 | 0 | 0–3 | |
| 13. Bob Tufts | 27 | 42 | 81 | 2 | 2–0 | |
| 14. Roger Samuels | 20 | 27 | 76 | 0 | 1–2 | |
| 15. Moe Savransky | 16 | 24 | 86 | 0 | 0–2 | |
| 16. Mike Milchin | 39 | 32.7 | 68 | 0 | 3–1 | |
| 17. Happy Foreman | 6 | 11.3 | 128 | 0 | 0–0 | |
| 18. Bud Swartz | 5 | 5.3 | 58 | 0 | 0–0 | |
| 19. Herb Karpel | 2 | 1.7 | 32 | 0 | 0–0 | |
| 20. Brian Bark | 3 | 2.3 | Infinity | 0 | 0–0 | |
| 21. Ed Wineapple | 1 | 4 | 94 | 0 | 0–0 | |

# 13

## Right-Handed Relievers

⚾

The talent level of Jewish right-handed relievers, as a whole, is not that deep. Twenty-six Jewish righty relievers have pitched in the big leagues; just three of them have logged as many as 300 innings. But just as clearly, the finest of any Jewish reliever, regardless of throwing hand, is Larry Sherry.

Sherry was, 50 years ago, the Joba Chamberlain of the Los Angeles Dodgers, a hard-throwing rookie who became the dominant relief pitcher in the latter part of the 1959 season. Unlike Chamberlain, Sherry got the chance to pitch in the World Series at the end of his rookie year and took home a World Series MVP award in the process.

Like Chamberlain, Sherry's dominance and varied repertoire led many to think his future was as a starter. Ulti-

*Larry Sherry*

mately, Sherry proved to be a far better reliever than starter, with just a 4.44 ERA in games he began, 3.55 in games he entered in the middle of the action. While that is within range for the expected ERA split between starter and reliever, early in his career, when he was in both roles, the numbers are stark. In 1959 Sherry posted a 3.10 ERA as a starter, 0.74 as a reliever. In 1960 he was at 5.56 as a starter, 3.46 as a reliever. And in 1961 he had a 3.40 ERA as a reliever—in his one start, he allowed 6 runs over 2 innings for an ERA of 27.00.

Al Levine is the other righty with a strong case: he posted six seasons with an ERA+ of 100 or better, as Sherry did, and his career ERA of 3.96, once adjusted for park and era, puts him at an ERA+ of 118. Sherry's career ERA+ was at 101. But Sherry pitched 799⅓ innings, while Levine logged just 575⅓, or roughly 30 percent fewer innings. Sherry's ERA+ also suffers for his time pitching half his games in Dodger Stadium, but his numbers were no stadium mirage—he actually fared better away from home in his career (3.54 ERA) than at home (3.79 ERA).

Sherry's numbers also suffer from his 16 starts, and though the two pitchers pitched in an identical number of games—416—Sherry provided more value to his teams in those games with his additional workload. Add in his value as measured by his contemporaries (not only the World Series MVP in 1959, but Sherry received a pair of MVP votes for his versatile 1960 season), and the battle isn't particularly close.

## 1. Larry Sherry

*Bats Right, Throws Right*
*Los Angeles Dodgers, 1958–1963*
*Detroit Tigers, 1964–1967*
*Houston Astros, 1967*
*California Angels, 1968*

In the Dodgers' defense, it is easy to see why it appeared that Larry Sherry had a chance to be a very fine major league starter. In 1957 Sherry led the Texas League in strikeouts as a starter, and he earned manager Walter Alston's praise in the spring of 1958.

"Stan Williams may be faster, but Sherry's fastball has more life," Alston said in the March 26, 1958, issue of *The Sporting News*. "He showed me some pretty good stuff and he's come up with a fine change-up—something Williams doesn't have at all." Considering that Williams went on to post a 3.56 ERA in 208 career starts, that Sherry was ahead of him developmentally says a lot.

Even Sherry's relief outings showed starter potential. His August 15, 1959, performance earned him prominent mention in *The Sporting News*' August 26, 1959, "Hats Off" column. Replacing an ineffective Johnny Podres with one out in the first, Sherry pitched 8²/₃ innings of scoreless relief for Los Angeles.

By the 1959 Series, Sherry's "backup slider" was being praised by Dodgers coach and former manager Charlie Dressen. And while his relief work in the 1959 World Series earned him, according to *The Sporting News*, "the Ed Sullivan show . . . two days later was on the Pat Boone Show," the Dodgers still tried to make him a starter.

Three other important notes about Sherry. He is a fine example of scouts over stats. In the minor leagues, his season as strikeout king in the Texas League was his only one with an ERA under 4.39. But the Dodgers clearly saw something in him that got him promoted after posting a 7.82 ERA in C-ball, a 4.90 ERA in B-ball, a 4.39 ERA in A-ball, and even a 4.91 ERA at AAA.

Sherry, as mentioned before, was a teammate of Barry Latman for Fairfax High School, which also produced Jewish catcher and Sherry's brother Norm Sherry. It is noteworthy that Sherry was one of the first Dodgers, therefore, to pitch in Los Angeles. He logged 20⅔ innings for Brooklyn's AAA farm team in Los Angeles, during Brooklyn's last season with the Dodgers.

One of my favorite aspects to Sherry's career is that he was born with club feet but overcame this. Did you know that Kristi Yamaguchi and Mia Hamm did as well? Clearly, we live in amazing medical times.

## 2. Al Levine
*Bats Left, Throws Right*
*Chicago White Sox, 1996–1997*
*Texas Rangers, 1998*
*Anaheim Angels, 1999–2002*
*Tampa Bay Devil Rays, 2003*
*Kansas City Royals, 2003*

*Detroit Tigers, 2004*
*San Francisco Giants, 2005*

There would have been a time when Al Levine's signing by the 2008 Newark Bears would have been hailed by a huge, vibrant Jewish community in the city. But the city, which once held 70,000 Jews and 50 different *shuls*, now has just one synagogue with a population of 300.

Still, between the Levine signing and the opening of the Jewish Museum of New Jersey in December 2007, perhaps Jews and Newark are reopening their long-dormant love affair.

More likely, however, is that both Jewish Newark and Al Levine's best days are in the past, though Levine did post a 1.84 ERA in his first 11 innings with the independent league Bears. Levine had been out of baseball for two years before returning in 2008 and has a career line worthy of praise.

The astounding thing about Levine's success is that he did it with an obscenely low strikeout rate. For his career, Levine struck out 4.4 batters per nine innings, which is among the lowest rates among modern relievers with his level of success. Nor did his walk rate stay extremely low— 3.7 is above average. And even his batting average against wasn't particularly impressive—.270 is good, but not great.

But that batting average against drops to .256 with runners in scoring position. With two outs and runners in scoring position, Levine's BAA falls to .220.

If there was such a thing as a purely clutch pitcher, Levine would be it. Coming through with runners on base is what propelled him to an ERA+ of 118.

### 3. Jose Bautista

*Bats Right, Throws Right*
*Baltimore Orioles, 1988–1991*
*Chicago Cubs, 1993–1994*
*San Francisco Giants, 1995–1996*
*Detroit Tigers, 1997*
*St. Louis Cardinals, 1997*

And the winner of the most unlikely moniker for a Jewish player is . . . Jose Bautista! He narrowly edges Ruben Amaro Jr. No conversion here, either; the product of a Dominican father and Jewish mother posted some sensational minor league seasons, along with a pair of terrific major league years in relief, and another seven that ranged from competent to less so.

Bautista was signed by the New York Mets in 1981 at the age of 16. The Mets brought him along slowly, and were rewarded for it, as Bautista put up a solid season in A-ball, 13–4, 3.13 ERA in 135 innings with Columbia in 1984. He followed it by going 15–8 with a 2.34 ERA for high-A Lynchburg. The Mets then chose to make him repeat Lynchburg, and his ERA rose to 3.94. But by 1987, he posted a 10–5, 3.24 ERA season in the all-important jump to AA Jackson. His strikeout rate showed he wasn't yet ready for the majors—95 in 169 innings pitched—but at 22, he was a solid prospect.

The Mets at that time were so overstuffed with young pitching that they could not protect Bautista on the 40-man roster, so the Baltimore Orioles plucked him away in the Rule V draft. The 1988 Orioles, of course, had no reason to avoid wasting a roster spot on Bautista—the team started 0–21, meaning they were out of contention by Tax Day. But Bautista was put to work, and he acquitted himself well. The 6–15 record is indicative of little other than that Baltimore was terrible. He posted an ERA of 4.30, good for an ERA+ of 91 and not bad for a rookie making the jump from AA.

Bautista spent the next three years on the AAA-MLB shuttle, gradually improving his walk rate at AAA Rochester and pitching decently for the Orioles as a fill-in starter and reliever. He signed with Kansas City in 1992 but failed to make the big league club.

But in 1993, the Cubs signed him, and he turned in one of the finest relief seasons any Jewish pitcher ever had. As a swingman, he pitched 111²/₃ innings of 2.82 ERA baseball, good for an ERA+ of 141. Though he struck out just 63, he was extremely stingy with walks, allowing just 27.

Bautista was good in 1994, though not as excellent as in 1993, posting a 3–4 record and 3.89 ERA. The performance earned him a two-year contract with the San Francisco Giants. By the bay, his performance suffered mightily in 1995—his ERA ballooned to 6.44—but recovered in 1996, as he posted a 3.36 ERA for a 121 ERA+.

Sadly, this turned out to be his last hurrah in the major leagues. After struggling in 1997 for both the Tigers (6.69 ERA) and Cardinals (6.57 ERA), Bautista finished his playing career with two nondescript seasons in the minors.

Overall, Bautista's career totals—a 4.62 ERA in 685²/₃ innings, good for an ERA+ of 87—don't really tell the tale.

Bautista was often much better than that. Unfortunately for him, just as often, he was much worse.

## 4. Scott Feldman

*Bats Left, Throws Right*
*Texas Rangers, 2005–*

One of the reasons the Texas Rangers were able to deal pitching phenomenon Edison Volquez for the slugger Josh Hamilton was a belief that Scott Feldman could become an effective major league starter.

In his first season, the returns were encouraging. Feldman posted a 5.18 ERA over 25 starts, and much of the damage to his ERA happened in his last few outings, when he reached an innings total he'd never approached in the minor leagues. Texas ignored its promise to limit Feldman to occasional relief the rest of the 2008 season, putting Feldman's future at risk. Still, Feldman could, with another three seasons of similar effectiveness, be moved to the starting pitcher list.

He's just 25, and both big and strong enough to make that jump. Feldman is 6'5", 210 pounds. He has a good sense of humor, and any Jewish fan should wish for his success. Sadly, the Rangers sport two of the best young Jewish players in Feldman and Ian Kinsler, but Arlington is not a huge Jewish stronghold.

While Kinsler is the bigger star, Feldman should hold the edge among Jewish moms. In a February 26, 2008, interview with the *Dallas News*, when asked what his long-term financial goals are, Feldman included in his desired luxuries, "I'd like to get a car for my mom."

Scott Feldman was well trained.

### 5. Sam Nahem
*Bats Right, Throws Right*
*Brooklyn Dodgers, 1938*
*St. Louis Cardinals, 1941*
*Philadelphia Phillies, 1942, 1948*

While Moe Berg gets the most attention among baseball's well-known intellectuals, attention should also be paid to Sam Nahem, who fit a major league career into a life filled with political and legal accomplishments.

Make no mistake about it: Nahem's politics did not help him to reach Moe Berg level fame. Nahem was a Communist, and at no point could that have made life in America easy for him. It didn't stop him from serving ably in World War II, and it didn't keep him from sustained major league success—walking too many batters did—although perhaps this was simply Nahem's way of sharing the wealth.

Nahem was a Brooklyn kid, and he signed with the Dodgers after completing his degree at Brooklyn College. By the time he was dealt to the St. Louis Cardinals in a trade that brought Ducky Medwick in return, Nahem had passed the New York Bar. But Nahem, like Berg, did not have the inclination to practice law.

"Time enough for the law," Nahem told *The Sporting News* on May 22, 1941, "after I make good in the big leagues." He went on to post a 2.98 ERA in 81²/₃ innings for the Cardinals, though he walked 38 and struck out just 31. But the Cards dealt him to Philadelphia. A year later, after posting a 4.94 ERA for the Phillies, Nahem entered the service and didn't reappear in the major leagues until 1948, when he closed out his career in Philadelphia. However, Nahem spent much of his service time playing baseball to entertain the troops in Europe.

Nahem was only 32 years old when he last pitched in the big leagues, and he had miles to go before he slept. He was not an observant Jew—his son Andrew, in Nahem's *San Francisco Chronicle* obituary, referred to Nahem and his brother as "atheists. My father rebelled against Hebrew school when he was 13," he said.

Culturally Jewish, Nahem lived the ideal life of the politically progressive Jew. He married an art student, had three children, and moved with his family to Berkeley, California, in 1964. He worked for Chevron Chemical, becoming a labor leader for the Oil, Chemical, and Atomic Workers of America.

According to his son Ivan, he said of Chevron, "We're all a bunch of intellectual Jews here, and we're supposed to be proletarians." Little wonder Nahem and his family loved the Marx Brothers.

In his retirement, he still volunteered at the University Art Museum, and his companion described his cooking in complimentary terms.

He may not have been the best pitcher in Jewish baseball history. Biblically speaking, perhaps he wasn't even the best Jew. But it is hard to imagine a better dinner companion in Jewish baseball history, with the possible exception of Moe Berg, than Sam Nahem.

## 6. Lloyd Allen
*Bats Right, Throws Right*
*California Angels, 1969–1973*
*Texas Rangers, 1973–1974*
*Chicago White Sox, 1974–1975*

The 1968 draft was top-heavy on Jews: both Dick Sharon and Lloyd Allen were among the first 12 picks. Unfortunately, both were relative disasters, particularly Allen, who put up some good minor league seasons but pitched to a 4.69 career ERA in 297 innings—an ERA+ of just 70.

Allen went 12th overall in 1968. Just five picks later, the Giants grabbed Gary Matthews. Thirteen picks after Allen, the Dodgers selected Bill Buckner. And 116 picks later, the Red Sox nabbed Cecil Cooper.

Allen had some stellar performances en route to the big leagues. In 1969 he pitched to a 2.27 ERA, with 126 strikeouts in 127 innings, for San Jose of the Class A California League. That earned him a brief call-up in 1969, a slightly longer one in 1970, and he arrived in the majors for real in 1971.

His first full season was extremely successful—94 innings and a 2.49 ERA, good for an ERA+ of 130. He struck out 72, walked 40. His 15 saves ranked seventh in the American League.

But the drop-off in Allen's performance in 1971 and afterward seems like it has to be at least partially due to injury. His ERA jumped to 3.48, which in the 1971 run environment meant an ERA+ of 84. He walked more batters than he struck out, and he fanned only 53 in 85$\frac{1}{3}$ innings. His 1972 was far worse—a 9.42 ERA, 39 ERA+, 44 walks in 49$\frac{2}{3}$ innings, just 29 strikeouts, and a trade to the Texas Rangers.

Nothing changed in Texas or, after being picked up by the White Sox, in Chicago, either. He seemed to recover some of his form in 1976 with AA Tulsa, winning 11 games and pitching to a 2.81 ERA, with the walks down to just 56 in 154 innings. But he didn't get another major league shot. He pitched another three minor league seasons—in 1977–1978, a total of just 30 innings. So it appears an injury eventually caught up with him.

As always, it is impossible to predict the future of pitching prospects. Few examples are starker than Lloyd Allen, who started so bright and finished with a career record of 8–25.

## 7. Al Schacht

*Bats Right, Throws Right*
*Washington Senators, 1919–1921*

Al Schacht belongs to an exclusive club: he is one of only three Clown Princes of Baseball recognized by the Baseball Hall of Fame.

Ralph Berger described Schacht's act in a SABR Biography Project: "He would come in with his battered top hat and ragged tails, blowing mightily on a tuba. Maybe he'd wield a catcher's mitt that weighed twenty-five pounds into which one could fit an entire meal. In fact, this zany guy once ate a meal off home plate."

Schacht is listed by Baseball-Reference.com at 5'11", 142 pounds, both of which appear to be generous, and still places Schacht as the 10th-lightest pitcher since 1901. But on pure will, Schacht battled his way through the minors and put up a season that no one would be ashamed of in 1919 for Jersey City of the then-AA International League—19–17, 1.95 ERA in 318 innings. The success finally got him a chance to play big league baseball with the Senators.

In all, his three seasons were fairly successful; though a collision at second base midway through the 1920 season supposedly ruined his arm, he still managed, after leaving the major leagues, to put up successful lines in a pair of minor league seasons. He finished with a 4.48 ERA in 186 major league innings with Washington, walking 61 and striking out 38. (Keep in mind that in 1921, only 10 pitchers had as many as 101 strikeouts.)

But Schacht became a performer for decades. During World War II, Schacht, according to Berger, did "159 stage shows, visited 72 hospitals and 230 wards, and traveled over 40,000 miles" in a two-month period. Then it was on to the Pacific theater. He performed at 25 World Series and wrote four books on the subject, including *Clowning through Baseball*.

For all his clowning, this clown is recognized as a Clown

Prince of Baseball by the Baseball Hall of Fame. But only Max Patkin (a Jewish minor league pitcher, by the way) of the Clown Princes of Baseball has been so honored by the International *Clown* Hall of Fame. Certainly, no fair-minded Clown Hall voter can claim with a straight face that Buttons the Clown, T. J. Tatters, and Bumpsy Anthony are all Clown of Famers, but Al Schacht isn't.

Surely there must be room in that Hall of Fame for this fine clown. When it comes to clowns, I'm not a small Hall guy. I want those doors to open, and for honorees to come out, one after another, in a seemingly endless parade. To deny Schacht admission is a shot of seltzer to the face of every clown-minded individual in America.

## 8. Wayne Rosenthal

*Bats Right, Throws Right*
*Texas Rangers, 1991–1992*

Of all the many pitchers who might have been, Wayne Rosenthal is among the most surprising misses. A big Brooklyn-born right-hander out of St. John's, Rosenthal was drafted in the 24th round by the Texas Rangers and needed to prove himself. He did, at every level, striking out more than a batter an inning at three different levels, including AAA. He put up full-season ERAs of 0.73, 1.70, and 2.05 and partial-season marks of 2.22 and 2.40.

But Rosenthal did not find that success in the major leagues. He put up a 1991 season with the Rangers of a 5.25

ERA in 70¹/₃ innings. His strikeout rate was good—7.8 per nine innings—but his walk rate was too high, at 4.6 per nine. And after a rough start in 1992, he was dispatched to AAA, where he posted a 5.69 ERA and was released. After posting a 4.80 ERA with Duluth-Superior of the independent Northern League, Rosenthal called it a career.

Rosenthal clearly had the ability to make hitters swing and miss, and he's knowledgeable enough about pitching to have served as the Marlins pitching coach for several years, currently holding the position of minor league pitching coordinator. On a team that rebuilds as often as the Marlins do, that's a critical position.

I suspect injury played a role here, but the truth is, it may simply be that talent and knowledge, for something as difficult as pitching in the major leagues, aren't always enough.

### 9. Alan Koch
*Bats Right, Throws Right*
*Detroit Tigers, 1963–1964*
*Washington Senators, 1964*

Alan Koch was part of the "New Breed" of baseball player, according to the March 13, 1965, issue of *The Sporting News.* Koch graduated from Auburn University, then returned during off-seasons to earn a master's degree in American history from Alabama.

The column goes on to note that not only did fellow Washington pitcher Jim Hannan have a master's degree in business administration, but "the Senators could rank as the most intellectual club in the majors" because coach Eddie Yost also had a master's degree in physical education.

Even this article sells the Senators short. Manager Gil Hodges was known as one of the smartest managers of his time. Second baseman John Kennedy's namesake won a Pulitzer Prize for the landmark book *Profiles in Courage* and guided us through the Cuban missile crisis (though the ball-playing Kennedy hit just .225 for his career). And nobody can approach the size of infielder Don Zimmer's head.

So how did the smartest team in baseball finish? Ninth place, 62–100. A little Nuke LaLoosh might have helped.

As for Koch, he was no Nuke, posting a 5.41 ERA over 128 career innings, good for an ERA+ of 70. Fortunately, he had a good education to fall back on.

## 10. Hy Cohen

*Bats Right, Throws Right*
*Chicago Cubs, 1955*

Hy Cohen's military service presented a different kind of challenge for his pitching development. Cohen posted a solid 16–10, 2.86 ERA season for Des Moines of the Class A Western League in 1951. But he missed 1952 and 1953 serving in the military.

When he returned, clearly his pitching prowess returned as well. Cohen won the Western League ERA title for Des Moines in 1954, pitching to a 1.88 ERA to go along with his

16–6 record. He walked 53, struck out 100, and in the mind of Don Newcombe, who had served with him, Cohen was ready for stardom.

"He's got more stuff than most major league pitchers right now," Newcombe said in the November 20, 1954, edition of *The Sporting News*. "His fast ball is wicked, his curve ball breaks very sharp and he has a more effective slider than most major leaguers. I'll be surprised if he isn't a consistent winner for the Cubs in 1955."

But to Newcombe's surprise, Cohen wasn't a consistent winner, though in his defense, he got only one start and six relief appearances before being sent down in June. His totals were uninspiring, however: 17 innings of 7.94 ERA pitching, 10 walks, and just 4 strikeouts. After being sent to Los Angeles of the Pacific Coast League, he was just 5–10 with a 3.59 ERA.

Now, part of this may be the jump from A-ball to the majors, and even the PCL was AAA. But after a two-year layoff, Cohen threw a lot of innings in 1954—a jump to nearly 200 innings from zero. That jump may well have affected his pitching. At the very least, 1955 was likely the worst season for Cohen to make an impression, on the heels of his 1954 total.

Cohen pitched several more seasons in the minor leagues, including a 1957 that saw him go 15–7, 2.72 ERA in the AA Southern Association for the Memphis Chicasaws. But despite some brutal Cub teams, Cohen never got a second chance.

## 11. Keith Glauber
*Bats Right, Throws Right*
*Cincinnati Reds, 1998, 2000*

Keith Glauber was a 42nd-round draft pick. He exceeded expectations by even making it to the major leagues. Only two of the 42nd-round picks logged big league time in 1994—only once in the decade of the '90s did more than two 42nd rounders make it, and five times in the decade, none of the 42nd rounders reached the promised land.

Glauber now runs the Young People's Day Camp (YPDC) in Staten Island, after a pair of shoulder surgeries ended his professional baseball career. His father is in charge of the whole enterprise, which stresses on its Web site that it is "more than just a day camp," though, based on the activities, trips, and counselors, it appears to be, in fact, just a day camp. But Glauber was more than just a 42nd-round draft pick prior to his injuries. Over eight minor league seasons, Glauber posted an ERA of 3.94, a strikeout rate of 7.25, and a walk rate of just 3.22. He allowed .66 home run per nine innings. And in a pair of call-ups, he took his game to another level.

In 15 major league innings, Glauber posted a 3.00 ERA, striking out eight and walking just three. He did not allow a home run, and his ERA+ for his major league tenure was 151. It isn't clear what else Cincinnati could have expected from him, or why he didn't receive more of a chance for Reds clubs that ranked 10th in the National League in ERA in 1998 and 5th in 2000. Unfortunately for Glauber, his performance suffered in 2001, when the Reds, 14th over-all in the National League in ERA, almost certainly would have called upon him.

This past summer, YPDC of Staten Island visited the Bronx Zoo, the Statue of Liberty, Ellis Island, the Staten Island Yankees, and even Medieval Times. But Keith Glauber's successful day trips to the major leagues will make even the likely triumphs of both Water Day and Crazy Hat Day pale in comparison.

### 12. Justin Wayne
*Bats Right, Throws Right*
*Florida Marlins, 2002–2004*

Justin Wayne presented me with a terrific dilemma when he made his major league debut on September 3, 2002.

I was in the stands at Shea Stadium, lured by the 2-for-1 doubleheader, as well as the promise of history. With a loss in the first game, the Mets had a chance to set the National League record for most consecutive home losses. It would be on my conscience forever if someday my grandchildren asked about that moment, and I told them I was elsewhere.

But after the record was set, the Mets faced Jewish pitcher Justin Wayne in the nightcap. And so my loyalties were set against one another: was I more of a Mets fan or more of a Jew?

Ultimately, perhaps my wardrobe decided for me—I had on my Mike Piazza jersey, but no *tefillin*. I decided on a rooting strategy that was, strictly speaking, a *shande* for the *goyim*. My reasoning was that Wayne, a top draft pick by the Marlins, had a bright future ahead of him. So when the Mets knocked him out after four innings, on the strength of home runs by Raul Gonzalez and Roberto Alomar, I decided to simply enjoy what was a rare positive offensive performance by my favorite team.

Unfortunately, the start was symptomatic of Wayne's difficulties in the major leagues. It should have been a red flag that if late-career Roberto Alomar could hit him, anybody could hit him. In 61 1/3 major league innings, Wayne posted a 6.13 ERA, with 36 walks and 37 strikeouts. He got hit hard as a starter (6.62 ERA) and as a reliever (5.53 ERA).

Oddly, even in the minor leagues, Wayne never approached his dominant strikeout numbers from his time at Stanford University. His K-rate ranged from 8.63 to 10.3 per nine innings as an undergrad, against top competition, but fell to 5.92 in his 547 minor league innings.

The economics major from Stanford should have no trouble making his way into the real world with baseball at an end. Perhaps he'll end up with a government job—he is an alum of Punahou High School in Honolulu, as is, of course, Barack Obama.

### 13. Ed Corey
*Bats Right, Throws Right*
*Chicago White Sox, 1918*
Like Roy Hobbs in *The Natural*, Ed Corey made it to the big leagues as a pitcher, pitched very briefly, then years later, surfaced as a minor league outfielder.

Also like Hobbs, Ed Corey was a successful minor league pitcher, with a 2.68 ERA in 59 innings for the AA Louisville Colonels in 1919 (though he did pitch to a mediocre 4.50 ERA in two big league innings).

But unlike Hobbs, Corey didn't get to play outfield in the major leagues. Topping out at AA, he failed to literally tear the cover off the ball with a hit, and as far as I know, he didn't get shot by some crazy lady in black.

## 14. Bob Davis
*Bats Right, Throws Right*
*Kansas City Athletics, 1958, 1960*

Sixty-one baseball players with the last name of Davis, and only one, Bob, was a member of the Jewish faith. Davis has been the name of Hall of Famers (George), All-Stars like Jody and Glenn, Alvins and Jumbos, Chili and Crash.

Other than his Judaism, Bob Davis's career doesn't stand out very much. Despite being a New York product, he appears to be the one player on the late '50s Athletics that the Yankees didn't acquire.

His best minor league season came in 1958 for AA Little Rock of the Southern Association. As the ace of the staff, he went 11–8 but pitched to a 2.17 ERA in 170 innings.

Davis had two major league seasons of approximately equal length. In 1958 he pitched to a 7.84 ERA in 32 innings. In 1960 he pitched to a 3.66 ERA in 31 innings. His total was 63 innings at 5.71 ERA. The lesson? It's tough to balance out a 7.84 ERA.

## 15. Harry Shuman
*Bats Right, Throws Right*
*Pittsburgh Pirates, 1942–1943*
*Philadelphia Phillies, 1944*

There is a story in *The Encyclopedia of Jews in Sports*, likely apocryphal, that Harry Shuman was signed to a contract after pitching batting practice as a lark for the Philadelphia Athletics while a Temple University law student. His throwing apparently impressed Connie Mack, who signed him to a minor league deal.

The story doesn't hold up, as Shuman was already in the minor leagues in 1936, not to mention just 21, making it somewhat unlikely that he was simultaneously in law school, too.

However he got started, Shuman took a few years to figure out how to pitch, but something changed for him between 1938, when he posted a 3–6 record and 6.24 ERA for the Class B Richmond Colts of the Piedmont League, and 1939, when his record for Richmond improved to 17–12. Two seasons later, an 18–6, 2.24 ERA campaign with the Class B Harrisburg Senators earned him a shot with the Pittsburgh Pirates in 1942.

Shuman, even in the talent-diluted World War II majors, didn't have much success in the major leagues. In 50²/₃ innings, his ERA was just 4.44, and he walked 20 while striking out just 10.

Still, the Philadelphia product got the chance to pitch for his hometown Phillies in 1944. But when the Phillies sold him to Los Angeles of the Pacific Coast League, he decided to stay in his hometown.

"We just had a baby and he was making about $700 a month," said his wife of 57 years, Phyllis Rendelman Shuman, in Shuman's *Philadelphia Inquirer* obit on October 27, 1996. "He was a very, very good family man."

Shuman went on to work in a number of city jobs, including supervisor of sales tax collection for the Department of Revenue, which is probably the only person who gets booed in Philadelphia more than the team's players.

## 16. Izzy Goldstein
*Bats Both, Throws Right*
*Detroit Tigers, 1932*

When Hank Greenberg posted a monster 1932 season for the Beaumont Explorers of the Texas League, winning the circuit's MVP award, a Jewish star in the Texas town was old hat, thanks to Izzy Goldstein.

Goldstein, one of the three players in the Odessa-to-major leagues pipeline, had been the star of the 1931 Beaumont team. Goldstein led the team in wins with 16, put up a solid 3.58 ERA, and even contributed seven doubles and three triples at the plate.

Considering that Beaumont's home run leader just two years earlier had been a man named Easterling, and a teammate of Goldstein's was named Christian, Goldstein likely stood out on that team, to say nothing of Beaumont's reputation for a small number of Jews.

W. T. Block wrote in an article entitled "A Brief History of the Early Beaumont Jewish Community," "Except for itinerant wagon peddlers, no other Jews are known to have arrived in Beaumont until 1878, when Morris J. Loeb moved his family here and opened a cigar store. Wolf Bluestein and J. Solinsky settled in Orange in 1876."

Sounds like with Goldstein and Greenberg, they were still short of a *minyan*.

Unfortunately, Goldstein did not make the transition to Detroit as well as Greenberg. Given a chance to both start and relieve for the Tigers in 1932, Goldstein pitched to a 4.47 ERA in 56$\frac{1}{3}$ innings, which was good for a solid 105 ERA+ in the hitting-heavy 1932 American League. But he walked 41 in 56$\frac{1}{3}$ innings and struck out just 14.

Goldstein pitched for the Toronto Maple Leafs of the International League in 1933, but his 9–7, 4.17 ERA season did not bring about a second major league trial.

Rob Edelman had a terrific line about Goldstein in an August 20, 2004, article in the *Forward* on Jewish baseball players that reflects the American Jewish experience: "He was born in 1908 in Odessa, pitched in 16 games for the 1932 Detroit Tigers and died in 1993 in Delray Beach, Fla."

### 17. Bill Hurst
*Bats Right, Throws Right*
*Florida Marlins, 1996*
A huge mound presence, 6'7" Bill Hurst got just two scoreless innings in the big leagues. He made his debut in Phila-

delphia on September 18, 1996, and he pitched a scoreless eighth inning. On September 28, he also posted a run-free eighth in Houston.

Just getting to the big leagues is a long shot for a 20th-round pick, which is what Hurst was by the Cardinals in 1989. That was a good round that year, however—10 picks later was Tim Worrell, a longtime relief pitcher, and 13 picks later was Jeff Kent, the standout second baseman.

Hurst showed little in the St. Louis organization, however, and the recently created Florida Marlins picked him up prior to the 1995 season. After a solid 1995 for the high-A Brevard County Manatees, he excelled in 1996 as the closer for AA Portland, saving 30 games and posting a 2.20 ERA in the Eastern League. That earned him his big league look.

But injuries appear to have derailed Hurst—his 1997 was a struggle, and by 1999 he was out of baseball.

### 18. Sid Schacht

*Bats Right, Throws Right*
*St. Louis Browns, 1950–1951*
*Boston Braves, 1951*

Sid Schacht, who got a late start in professional baseball, almost certainly due in part to World War II, followed by an extended illness of his mother's, was a tremendous minor league pitcher who got absolutely rocked in his brief major league travels.

Schacht began his minor league career at age 29 with the Stamford Bombers of the Class B Colonial League, and he immediately had huge success. He went 18–7 with a 2.94 ERA in 190 innings. Repeating the level in 1948, Schacht improved to a 2.09 ERA. Moved up to the Eastern League in 1949, he had his best season, 19–5, a 2.44 ERA, and just 59 walks in 181 innings.

A fine spring earned him a spot on the 1950 Browns roster, and this write-up in the March 29, 1950, issue of *The Sporting News*, under the headline "Another Chucking Schacht":

> He doesn't fit the pitchers' physical tape measure and he lacks the blow-'em-down fastball baseball men like to see, but rookie right-hander Sidney Schacht stands a strong chance to make the Browns' hill staff on his strong spring showing.
>
> Poise and control, seldom seen in a young hurler, have caught the experienced eye of manager Zach Taylor.

The article then details such spring feats as striking out Ralph Kiner on three pitches.

Unfortunately, as spring turned to summer, Schacht's strikeouts turned to walks. He posted a 16.03 ERA over eight games, including a start, and was soon dispatched to the Kansas City Blues of the American Association for more seasoning. Of course, he was already 32.

Returning in 1951, Schacht still couldn't get anybody out as a Brown, posting a 21.00 ERA. He was better for Boston after the Braves grabbed him off waivers on May 13, but despite a 1.93 ERA in 4²/₃ innings, he accumulated two losses. Sent back to Milwaukee of the American Association, he finished 4–1, 4.09 ERA, and called it a career.

Schacht's career major league totals are ugly: 21²/₃ innings, 21 walks, 12 strikeouts, a 14.34 ERA, good for an ERA+ of 31. In the minors, it is a different story: 55–29 career record, 2.84 ERA. That disparity, and the small sample size, leads me to believe Schacht, with more time, would have had more big league success. It is fair to point out, however, that he would have been hard-pressed to have less.

### 19. Moxie Manuel

*Bats Right, Throws Right*
*Washington Senators, 1905*
*Chicago White Sox, 1908*

Of the four baseball Moxies, this is the only Jewish Moxie (and I only hope it was said with affection, as in, "You have some moxie, kid, as a Jew playing much of your career in the turn-of-the-century South!").

Manuel made his professional debut in 1903 at age 22 for the Class D Vicksburg Hill Billies (no, seriously) of the Cotton States League. He went 14–12 and returned in 1904, improving to 21–11.

Promoted to the Class A Southern Association, he went just 6–8 for New Orleans in 1905, but he earned his first shot at major league time that September anyway. He pitched to a 5.40 ERA in 10 innings for the Washington Senators, walking three and striking out three. In a depressed offensive year, that meant an ERA+ of 49.

But his name wasn't Give Up Easily Manuel. It wasn't Sigh of Resignation Manuel. So he returned to New Orleans in 1906 and improved his record to 17–15. He jumped to 20–11 in 1907 and, according to *The Big Book of Jewish Baseball*, even pitched to some left-handed batters with his left hand. An ambidextrous pitcher—what moxie! That was good enough to get him another big league shot, this time with the White Sox.

Playing alongside fellow Jewish ballplayer Jake Atz, Manuel was the primary reliever for the White Sox in 1908. But on a team with 107 complete games, this doesn't provide as much work as one might expect 100 years later. Manuel even threw three complete games himself, yet totaled just 18 games and 60⅓ innings. He pitched to a 3.28 ERA, which sounds very good, but in 1908 offensive terms (the league average ERA was 2.31), it puts his ERA+ at 71. He walked 25 and struck out 25.

Clearly not sufficiently impressed, the Sox let Manuel head to Birmingham of the Southern Association, where he played in the minor leagues and never made it back to the big show.

And though he went just 11–18 in 1909 for Birmingham, Moxie Manuel didn't throw in the towel. He wasn't called Easily Surrenderable Manuel, somewhat because *surrenderable* isn't a word, but mostly because he had moxie.

So in 1910, Manuel went 18–14. And though he went 1–4 in 1911, he didn't get another major league call. And there is no record of Manuel pitching in professional base-ball after that.

Sometimes, you need more than moxie. You need a team that values moxie. In 1912 the Cleveland Indians needed some: they signed Moxie Meixell. They needed moxie. And they also needed an outfielder.

### 20. Steve Wapnick

*Bats Right, Throws Right*
*Detroit Tigers, 1990*
*Chicago White Sox, 1991*

Steve Wapnick, it must be said, played *Let's Make a Deal* with the Major League Baseball draft—and lost badly. He started with the car and ended up with the bag of popcorn.

He was drafted in the second round of the January 1985 draft (the draft was divided into January and June phases then) by the Padres—but didn't sign. He was then drafted in the fifth round of the June 1985 draft by the Athletics—but didn't sign. In 1987 he was drafted in the 30th round by the Blue Jays, and signed at last. I'd have cut my losses, too.

The sad thing is that the Blue Jays had a real steal in Wapnick, but an arm injury ruined what should have been a solid career as a major league reliever. Wapnick dominated at every level, putting up ERAs of 3.02, 2.05, and 2.24 in his first three minor league seasons to go with strikeout rates of 8.63, 10.29, and 8.05. Promoted to AA, he posted an ERA of 0.49. Sent to AAA, his ERA jumped—to 0.69.

But the Blue Jays hadn't put Wapnick on the 40-man

roster, and Detroit tried to stash him on the major league roster for a year. Wapnick's control deserted him there, and after 7 innings, 6 strikeouts, but 10 walks—leading to a 6.43 ERA—Wapnick was returned to the Toronto system.

He had a solid 1991 season for AAA Syracuse, with a 2.76 ERA and 58 strikeouts in 71²/₃ innings against just 25 walks. That led to the White Sox asking for him in a trade for Cory Snyder. In five late-1991 innings for the Sox, Wapnick's control abandoned him again—he had four walks in those five innings—but entering his age-26 season, his future appeared bright.

Sadly, injury seems to have curtailed his career. He didn't make the 1992 White Sox, and put up subpar numbers at AAA—in 71¹/₃ innings, he walked 48 hitters, striking out 59, and put up a 4.42 ERA. Signed by the Seattle Mariners, he put up worse numbers for AAA Calgary; his walks dropped, but his strikeouts dropped more, and the ERA rose to 4.96. At that point, Wapnick called it a career.

### 21. Conrad Cardinal
*Bats Right, Throws Right*
*Houston Colt .45s, 1963*
Expansion teams take different approaches. The New York Mets, born in 1962, decided to bring back as many familiar New York names as possible, with Gil Hodges, Duke Snider, Don Zimmer, and others on the roster during the team's first few seasons.

The Colt .45s, meanwhile, seemed to come up with a different plan, one that included this: let's stockpile young, untested Jewish arms. Conrad Cardinal was step 1 in this master plan.

It's hard to say either approach was a success. The Mets lost 100 or more games each of the team's first four years. The Colt .45s, who became the Astros in 1964, never lost 100 games, but they failed to win the National League West until 1980.

The Brooklyn-born Cardinal was grabbed by Houston first, after a solid first professional season with Jamestown of the New York–Penn League. Cardinal went 14–7, with a 3.74 ERA in Class D ball. Houston signed him, and by April 21, 1963, he was making a start for Houston.

Needless to say, the jump from Class D to the majors didn't go well. Cardinal did not make it out of the first inning in his only major league start, and he gave up runs in five of his six major league appearances. This is unfair to put on him, however—no organization should promote a kid from Class D to the majors. In $13^{1}/_{3}$ innings, his ERA was 6.08 (an ERA+ of 52), and he matched his 7 strikeouts with 7 walks.

Cardinal returned to the Texas League, which still represented a huge jump—D-ball to AA. He was decent, with a 4.26 ERA for San Antonio to go with a 9–9 record. Sent down to A-ball, with one can imagine a complete lack of confidence, he pitched poorly and by 1965 was out of baseball.

## 22. Larry Yellen

*Bats Right, Throws Right*
*Houston Colt .45s, 1963–1964*

Buoyed by this success, the Colt .45s decided when they signed Larry Yellen to have him essentially skip the minor leagues altogether. With just 99 innings with San Antonio under his belt—good ones, a 2.82 ERA, 74 strikeouts— Yellen got a September 26, 1963, start. He pitched pretty well, too: five solid innings, two earned runs, one walk, three strikeouts—against a Pittsburgh lineup that featured Roberto Clemente, Willie Stargell, and Donn Clendenon.

Suitably impressed, Houston decided to keep him with the big club in 1964. But Yellen just wasn't ready. In 21 innings, he walked 10, struck out just 9, and posted a 6.86 ERA (an ERA+ of 50). Sent to the Oklahoma City 89ers of the Pacific Coast League, then to Amarillo of the Texas League, Yellen never again found the form that led the Colt .45s to originally rush him. By 1965 Yellen, too, had thrown his last pitch.

Look, any team that decides to stock the roster with Jews is okay by me. What the Colt .45s hoped to gain from this is unclear. Their rushing of young position players—which included Jewish third baseman Steve Hertz—did not prevent players like Joe Morgan, Rusty Staub, and Jerry Grote from extended major league success. But pitchers, as the stories in this text and everywhere else will make clear, need to be handled carefully. It is worth wondering what Yellen and Cardinal could have been with a slow, steady developmental process.

## 23. Steve Ratzer
*Bats Right, Throws Right*
*Montreal Expos, 1980–1981*

Steve Ratzer was a pitcher with fantastic control that saw his career minor league numbers, and quite possibly his best shots at the major leagues, compromised by playing the majority of his time in the thin air of Denver.

After playing at St. John's University, Ratzer signed with the Montreal Expos as an undrafted free agent. He quickly made good use of his ticket to professional baseball, climbing from rookie ball to AA in the span of two years. His numbers were stellar at each level, including 73 innings of 1.48 ERA pitching with AA Quebec City of the Eastern League.

Then Ratzer met Denver, where Montreal had its AAA farm team. In 1978 Ratzer posted a 7–10 record, 5.00 ERA in the Rocky Mountains. But let's put those numbers in context. Bryn Smith, who went on to a solid major league career, put up a 6.83 ERA in 1978 for Denver. Scott Sanderson, another solid major league pitcher, came in at 6.06. Need more? All but one regular in the Denver lineup had an OPS of .778 or better—and so did four bench players.

Ratzer spent three full years in Denver, improving each season, before he got a chance to pitch for Montreal. The key was his walk rate, or lack thereof. He was at 1.96 walks per nine innings in his minor league career, but he dropped that number to 1.64 in his time with Denver. By 1980 he posted a 15–4 record, 3.59 ERA.

But Ratzer, whose time in the major leagues lasted from October 1980 to May 1981, did not bring that walk rate up with him. In his 21$^1$/$_3$ career innings with the Expos, Ratzer walked 9, struck out just 4, and had a lifetime ERA of 7.17, good for an ERA+ of 49. Sent back to Denver, he continued to keep the walks down. But with a surplus of pitchers, Montreal traded Ratzer to the Mets for infielder Frank Taveras.

How Ratzer didn't get a shot with the 1982 Mets is utterly beyond me. While he posted an 11–7, 3.08 ERA season for AAA Tidewater, the big club lost 97 games thanks mostly to a brutal pitching staff that ranked 11th in the National League in ERA.

Picked up by the White Sox for 1983, he was assigned to AAA . . . which meant a trip back to Denver! His walk rate was again terrific—just 16 in 61$^2$/$_3$ innings—but his home run rate shot way up, and he posted a 6.75 ERA. How much of that was luck? Probably a lot. But it turned out to be his last season in baseball.

According to *The Big Book of Jewish Baseball*, Ratzer retired and raised his family in Denver. Can you imagine? This is like Napoleon buying into an over-55 community at Waterloo.

## 24. Duke Markell
*Bats Right, Throws Right*
*St. Louis Browns, 1951*
Second only to Henry Bostick among the best gentile con-

versions of Jewish names is Duke Markell, born Harry Markowsky. But his middle name was Duquesne, and he came by the French honestly, born in Paris, France, one of eight major leaguers from the City of Lights.

As a result, Markell could never be president of the United States, but he filled plenty of other roles. Markell was an International League ace, a police officer, and a union agitator—which can't have helped his cause as he tried to get regular major league work.

Markell began his career with the Class D Hickory Rebels, posting a 5–2, 2.83 ERA season in 1945 over 82 innings. He broke out with a 19–9 record, 3.51 ERA in 1947 for Seaford of the Class D Eastern Shore League, but despite his solid efforts, he could get no higher than the Class A Utica Blue Sox for the remainder of the decade. Finally, after another 19-win season for the Class B Portsmouth Cubs, Markell got a chance to pitch for the AA Texas League Oklahoma City Indians. His 13–19 record obscured a 2.77 ERA, and the pitching-starved Browns picked Markell up near the end of the 1951 season.

Markell got into five games, including two starts for the Browns. But like Sid Schacht earlier in the 1951 season, Markell did not come through on behalf of the Jews for the Browns. In 21$\frac{1}{3}$ innings, Markell walked 20, struck out 10, and pitched to a 6.33 ERA, good for an ERA+ of 69.

So Markell returned to the minor leagues, and in his first exposure to AAA in 1952, he won 14 games for the Toronto

Maple Leafs and led the International League in strikeouts with 120. Markell went on to post ERAs under 4.00 in four of the five years he spent in the International League, winning 56 games in those five years.

Along the way, he got another chance. The Phils signed him for the 1954 season and gave him a chance to make the starting staff in the spring.

"I am sure I can win for the Phillies," Markell said in the December 30, 1953, issue of *The Sporting News*. "Maybe it sounds like boasting, but I feel I can take my place behind Robin Roberts and Curt Simmons and win my share of games." Instead, the fifth starter spot went to the forgettable Bob Miller. How forgettable? You know the Bob Millers on the 1962 Mets? Bob "Lefty" Miller and Bob "Righty" Miller? This Bob Miller wasn't either of those Bob Millers.

Markell's lack of fear is unsurprising, since in the off-season, he patrolled the Bronx as a police officer. And Markell didn't mind speaking up. As he told *The Sporting News* in the January 13, 1954, issue, "If I don't make it with the Phillies, I'm going to hang up my glove and quite baseball."

Instead, he kept on pitching and logged his third no-hitter by 1955. But by 1957, with his skills waning, Markell spoke out publicly about the fact that minor league players had no pension system.

"We realize it might be tougher for us to get pension money than it was for the big leaguers," Markell said in the May 8, 1957, issue of *The Sporting News*. "But we're convinced it could be done. Naturally, we don't expect to get as much as the major leaguers do."

Markell did not accomplish this (minor leaguers still don't have a pension), but his willingness to speak out was remarkable. Most remarkable of all were his inspirational abilities.

According to *The Sporting News*, Markell became a hero while pitching for Portsmouth, Virginia, in 1950, and "his swarthy features enabled most of the townspeople to spot him at a glance." ("I reckon that there's the Jew!" I imagine they said.)

"One night Markell was eating in a restaurant when he became conscious of a pair of eyes staring at him. He looked up and saw a small girl ignoring her food to look at her hero.

"The food grew colder and colder until finally the girl's mother walked over to Markell.

"'She won't touch her dinner,' the mother explained, 'and there's nothing I can do. Would you please come over and tell her to eat?'

"Markell did. The girl promptly finished her meal."

No one who was raised by a Jewish mother can doubt this account for a second.

## 25. Hal Schacker
*Bats Right, Throws Right*
*Boston Braves, 1945*
On the strength of an 18–7, 2.97 ERA season for Class A Hartford of the Eastern League in 1944, Hal Schacker

got the chance to pitch for the 1945 Boston Braves. But even in the diluted wartime National League, things did not go well for Schacker. In 15$\frac{1}{3}$ innings, Schacker walked 9, struck out 6, and pitched to a 5.28 ERA, an ERA+ of 73.

Schacker was just 20 and probably figured he'd get another chance once he paid his dues. Unfortunately, he never did. On the strength of a 20–7, 2.93 ERA season in 1948 for St. Petersburg of the Class C Florida International League, he was mentioned as a possible A's prospect for 1949 by *The Sporting News*.

"Connie [Mack], who took Schacker on the recommendation of [scout] Lou Finney, was impressed with his new pitcher's physique. Schacker, who pitched last winter in the Panama League, stands six feet, weighs 195 pounds, and is only 23 years old."

But Schacker didn't stick with the A's. Returning to the Florida International League, he posted a 2.75 ERA in 177 innings in 1949, but his record dropped to 9–9, which probably hurt his chances to advance. He pitched 1950 in the Class C Provincial League, splitting his time between St. Hyacinthe and Sherbrooke, and probably realizing how far he was from the big leagues, retired at 25.

I hope he enjoyed his brief time in the major leagues. He won 72 games in the minor leagues by age 25. But I'll bet he remembers those 15$\frac{1}{3}$ major league innings the most.

## 26. Cy Malis
*Bats Right, Throws Right*
*Philadelphia Phillies, 1934*

How can they possibly have an *E! True Hollywood Story* for Herve Villechaize (highly recommended, by the way, for the video shot of him dancing in a tuxedo with two Playboy bunnies), but not one for Cy Malis?

Malis played major league ball. He served in World War II, sustaining wounds that led to a morphine addiction. His doctors gave him alcohol to help him off the morphine. Guess what he got addicted to next?

He appeared in 37 movies and television shows and went on to found Narcotics Anonymous, helping many others after him fight addiction. And he even was a stand-in for a Stooge! (According to Stoogeworld.com, it was for Larry.)

I guess there aren't any good dancing midget videos to help E! tell the story. And that is a shame.

Malis only pitched a bit above Class D ball, with Philadelphia signing him in 1934, hoping that a hometown boy would make good. He allowed 2 runs in $3\frac{2}{3}$ innings in relief on August 17, 1934. He walked two and struck out one. The Phils lost to Paul Dean and the Cardinals, 12–2.

---

**TOP 11 CY MALIS FILMS, AS VOTED BY IMDB.COM USERS:**

1. *Night Editor*
2. *Somebody Up There Likes Me*
3. *Destination Tokyo*

4. *The Undercover Man*
5. *Framed*
6. *Johnny O'Clock*
7. *Dangerous Business*
8. *The Court-Martial of Billy Marshall*
9. *The Fuller Brush Girl*
10. *Around the World in 80 Days*
11. *Designing Woman*

| NAME | GAMES | INNINGS | ERA+ | SAVES | W-L | Additional |
|------|-------|---------|------|-------|-----|------------|
| 1. Larry Sherry | 416 | 799.3 | 101 | 82 MVP | 53–44 | 1959 WS |
| 2. Al Levine | 416 | 575.3 | 118 | 10 | 24–33 | |
| 3. Jose Bautista | 312 | 685.7 | 87 | 3 | 32–42 | |
| 4. Scott Feldman | 101 | 241 | 89 | 0 | 7–13 | |
| 5. Sam Nahem | 90 | 224.3 | 78 | 1 | 10–8 | |
| 6. Lloyd Allen | 159 | 297.3 | 70 | 22 | 8–25 | 1971: 2.49 ERA, 15 SV |
| 7. Al Schacht | 53 | 197 | 86 | 2 | 14–10 | |
| 8. Wayne Rosenthal | 42 | 75 | 75 | 1 | 1–4 | |
| 9. Alan Koch | 42 | 128 | 68 | 0 | 4–11 | |
| 10. Hy Cohen | 7 | 17 | 52 | 0 | 0–0 | 1954: 1.88 ERA in minors |
| 11. Keith Glauber | 7 | 15 | 151 | 0 | 0–0 | |
| 12. Justin Wayne | 26 | 61.7 | 67 | 0 | 5–8 | |
| 13. Ed Corey | 1 | 2 | 60 | 0 | 0–0 | 1919: 2.68 ERA in minors |
| 14. Bob Davis | 29 | 63 | 69 | 1 | 0–4 | |
| 15. Harry Shuman | 30 | 50.7 | 80 | 0 | 0–0 | |
| 16. Izzy Goldstein | 16 | 56.3 | 105 | 0 | 3–2 | |
| 17. Bill Hurst | 2 | 2 | Infinity | 0 | 0–0 | |
| 18. Sid Schacht | 19 | 21.3 | 31 | 1 | 0–2 | |

| NAME | GAMES | INNINGS | ERA+ | SAVES | W-L | Additional |
|------|-------|---------|------|-------|-----|------------|
| 19. Moxie Manuel | 21 | 70.3 | 66 | 1 | 3–4 | |
| 20. Steve Wapnick | 10 | 12 | 89 | 0 | 0–1 | |
| 21. Conrad Cardinal | 6 | 13.3 | 52 | 0 | 0–1 | |
| 22. Larry Yellen | 14 | 26 | 54 | 0 | 0–0 | |
| 23. Steve Ratzer | 13 | 21.3 | 49 | 0 | 1–1 | |
| 24. Duke Markell | 5 | 21.3 | 69 | 0 | 1–1 | |
| 25. Hal Schacker | 6 | 15.3 | 73 | 0 | 0–1 | |
| 26. Cy Malis | 1 | 3.7 | 96 | 0 | 0–0 | |

# 14

## The All-Time Jewish Team: Unbeatable

### ROSTER

C Harry Danning 1939
1B Hank Greenberg 1938
2B Buddy Myer 1935
3B Al Rosen 1953
SS Lou Boudreau 1948
LF Sid Gordon 1950
CF Elliott Maddox 1974
RF Shawn Green 2001

### BENCH

C Mike Lieberthal 1999
1B Mike Epstein 1969

2B Ian Kinsler 2007
1B/3B Kevin Youkilis 2007
OF Art Shamsky 1969
OF Goody Rosen 1945

---

## STARTING PITCHERS

---

Sandy Koufax 1966

Barney Pelty 1906

Ken Holtzman 1973

Erskine Mayer 1915

Steve Stone 1980

---

## RELIEF PITCHERS

---

Dave Roberts 1971
Saul Rogovin 1951
Jose Bautista 1993
Al Levine 2001
Scott Radinsky 1996
Larry Sherry 1959

According to the baseball statistician Konstantin Medvedovsky, this team, in a neutral environment, would score 1,067 runs and allow just 472. What does this mean? It means that in any league, the Jewish All-Stars would absolutely dominate.

Let's start with offensive prowess. The 1,067 runs ties the 1931 Yankees for the highest run total since 1900. That team was one of just seven teams since 1900 to score

1,000 runs: the 1930 Cardinals, 1930 Yankees, 1931 Yankees, 1932 Yankees, 1936 Yankees, 1950 Red Sox, and 1999 Indians. Only the 1930 and 1931 Yankees failed to make the playoffs, due to two extremely strong years by the Philadelphia Athletics—but the Yankees won 94 and 86 games in those seasons.

What kept these two New York teams from succeeding? Pitching. In 1931 the Yankees allowed 760 runs, which translated to a 4.20 ERA—third in the American League. The Athletics allowed 626 runs, which translated to a 3.47 ERA. In 1930 the Yankees' staff was flat-out mediocre, allowing 898 runs, sixth in the American League, and posting a 4.88 ERA.

Keep in mind also that these teams played in some of the most favorable run environments, while the Jewish team would score 1,067 runs in a neutral environment. Hence, the most similar offensive team would be the 1950 Red Sox, who posted 1,027 runs in a less-than-ideal offensive environment era-wise, though Fenway Park played as a huge hitter's park.

That team got a career year from Walt Dropo at first base (.322/.378/.583). Bobby Doerr had 27 home runs and 120 RBI at second base. Johnny Pesky's OBP at third base was .437. Vern Stephens at shortstop was an obscene .295/.361/.511. Even lesser offensive players like Dom DiMaggio (.328/.414/.452), Birdie Tebbetts (.310/.377/.444), and Al Zarilla (.325/.423/.493) were forces. Oh, and the other offensive starter was some guy named Ted Williams, who actually was well below his career numbers at a paltry .317/.452/.647.

The Jewish team outscored this team by 40 runs.

Now let's compare the Jewish team's pitching performance to the best of all time. The Jewish team allowed 472 runs. That is an absurdly low number in a neutral environment. To find competitors, one has to look to teams in some of the most run-depressed eras. Let's go to 1968, which is informally known as the Year of the Pitcher. Bob Gibson posted a 1.12 ERA, and Denny McLain won 31 games. The Baltimore Orioles allowed 497 runs; the Detroit Tigers allowed 492 runs. The two teams finished 1–2 in the 1968 American League race—the Tigers won it all. The difference between these two and the Jewish team? Detroit, the champion, scored 671 runs, while Baltimore checked in at 579. In other words, the two teams *combined* scored just 183 more runs than the Jewish team alone.

And it is no different when compared to the other great pitching staffs. The Atlanta Braves in 1995, in a strike-shortened season, allowed 540 runs. The 1986 Mets allowed 578 runs. The 1954 Cleveland Indians checked in at 504 runs. Even the 1966 Dodgers, who got the full advantage of the same Sandy Koufax career season the Jewish All-Star team has, allowed 490 runs.

So what does this mean? Based on the Pythagorean won-loss record, which converts runs scored and runs allowed into a likely record, the Jewish team would post a 135–27 record—an .833 winning percentage. This would easily be the finest season in baseball history. The 1906 Chicago Cubs were 116–36, a .763 winning percentage. They'd have finished far behind the Jewish team. Ditto the 1998 Yankees (114–48), the 1954 Indians (111–43), the 1986 Mets (108–54), and any other outfit in baseball history.

Make no mistake, this team would have been by far the greatest baseball has ever seen.

Let this set of statistics, and indeed, this book, ring out in response to the well-known *Airplane!* gag about Jewish athletes. In baseball alone, they are more than just a pamphlet. I encourage you, should anyone make that joke to you—throw this book at them. And I don't mean rhetorically. Actually throw this book at them and say, "Does this feel like a pamphlet? Well? Does it?"

As for those who take issue with the rankings in this book, I say: good. Let the discussion commence.

# GLOSSARY

**adjusted for era:** a statistic that normalizes any raw statistical advantages provided by the offensive or pitching advantages of the time in which that player played

**adjusted for park:** a statistic that normalizes any raw statistical advantages provided by that player's home ballpark

**batting average:** hits divided by at bats*

**batting line:** batting average/on-base percentage/slugging percentage, used as shorthand to express raw offensive value of a particular player

**clutch hitting:** hitting in important situations

**cup of coffee:** a brief time in the big leagues

**deadball era:** period in baseball, prior to 1920, when home runs were always scarce, and runs often were as well

---

* Batting average, on-base percentage, and slugging percentage are often cited shorthand as AVG/OBP/SLG. In Hank Greenberg's 1938 season, for example, his season line (batting average/on-base percentage/slugging percentage) can be expressed as .315/.438/.683.

**DERA:** a measure of ERA, as developed by Baseball Prospectus, that eliminates defensive contributions from a pitcher's performance

**Diaspora:** Jews living outside Israel

**EQA:** equivalent average, a Baseball Prospectus statistic that measures offensive contribution, expressed like a batting average (.260 is average, .300 is very good, etc.)

**ERA:** average earned runs allowed by a pitcher per nine innings

**ERA+:** statistic that adjusts a raw ERA for park and era and expresses it relative to the league average, with 100 being average and 105, for instance, 5 percent better than the league average

**fungo:** a practice flyball, usually hit by coaches to outfielders prior to a game

**Gold Glove:** annual award given by the Baseball Writers' Association of America to one player at each position in the National League and American League who is considered the best defender

**gridiron:** slang term for football

**hitter's park:** a park that tilts any performance toward hitters in that park

**innings eater:** a usually mediocre pitcher who provides extra value by pitching lots of innings

**International League:** a AAA minor league operating in the eastern United States

**James, Bill:** credited with founding the modern sabermetric movement

**Jewish Major Leaguers Baseball Card Set:** an annual treasure released by Martin Abramowitz and Jewish Major Leaguers, Inc., a Boston nonprofit dedicated to "documenting American Jews in America's game"

**major leagues:** the two main leagues of professional baseball in the United States: the National League and the American League

**minor leagues:** professional clubs owned by or affiliated with major league clubs; leagues are ranked from most challenging to least challenging, as follows: AAA (triple-A; one step below major league), AA (double-A), A (single-A; sometimes high-A, which is better competition than low-A), B, C, and D

**no-decision:** a start in which the pitcher receives neither a victory nor a loss

**on-base percentage:** times reaching base for any reason other than a fielding error, fielder's choice, dropped third strike, fielder's obstruction, or catcher's interference divided by plate appearances

**OPS:** short for on-base plus slugging percentage, a measure of a player's ability to get on base and hit for power

**OPS+:** a measure of on-base plus slugging percentage, adjusted for park and era, and expressed as a percentage of average production, with 100 being average, above 100 better than average

**Pacific Coast League (PCL):** a AAA minor league operating in the West and Midwest in the United States

**pitcher's park:** a park that tilts any performance toward pitchers in that park

**Pythagorean won-loss record:** converts runs scored and runs allowed into an expected record for that team

**range factor:** a defensive statistic, measuring the amount of ground a defensive player covers

**RBI:** short for runs batted in; runners on base driven home by a player's hit, walk, sacrifice fly, hit by pitch, or out that is not a double-play

**Rule V draft:** allows major league teams to select anyone not on another team's 40-man roster, with the proviso that the team must keep the player on the major league team all season or offer the player back to his original team

**sabermetrics:** the study of baseball through historical and statistical lenses, named for the Society for American Baseball Research (SABR)

**SABR Biography Project:** an ongoing effort to produce comprehensive biographical articles on "every person who ever played or managed in the major leagues, as well as any other person who touched baseball in a significant way"; the project is run by the Bioproject Committee of the Society for American Baseball Research

**slugging percentage:** number of total bases divided by at bats; used to measure a hitter's power

**WARP3:** Baseball Prospectus statistic, meaning "wins above replacement player"; it measures how many victories a team will have by playing a particular player at a position over a replacement-level player, and that value is normalized for park and era effects

# INDEX